DINOSAUR
COLLECTIBLES

ANTIQUE TRADER BOOKS

A DIVISION OF KRAUSE PUBLICATIONS

NORFOLK, VIRGINIA

DEDICATION

This one is for my brother

Doran Scott Adams

We made dinosaur villages and watched *The Valley of Gwangi* and *One Million Years B.C.* together as kids during the 1960s. Later, Doran became a geologist, and graduated from digging miniature caves in the dirt to play with, to actually digging up real dinosaurs.

—Dana Cain

For my beautiful wife Judith who always puts up with my collecting.

—Mike Fredericks

ISBN: 0-930625-99-4
Library of Congress Catalog Card Number: 98-071055

Editors: Allan W. Miller and Sandra Holcombe
Assistant Editors: Wendy Chia-Klesch and Marshall McClure
Production Assistants: Marshall McClure and Barbara Woerner
Art Director/Cover: Chris Decker
Graphic Artist: Jeff Hellerman

For a complete catalog of Antique Trader Books and to learn more about our other publications for collectors, please contact:
Antique Trader Publications
P.O. Box 1050
Dubuque, IA 52004
1-800-334-7165

CONTENTS

ACKNOWLEDGMENTS

Jack Arata • Brentwood, California
Evelyn Caldwell • Conifer, Colorado
Tony Campagna • Monticello, Arkansas
Kent Cordray, "Mr. Atomic" • Denver, Colorado
Lucinda Crecca • Englewood, Colorado
Cretaceous Creations • St. Louis, Missouri
William Daniel • Arvada, Colorado
Allen Debus • Bartlett, Illinois
Joe DeMarco • West Mifflin, Pennsylvania
Dinosaur National Monument • Colorado/Utah
Mike Evans • Cleburne, Texas
Jerry Finney • Lakewood, California
John Fischner • Needville, Texas
Flintstones Bedrock City • Custer, South Dakota
Shane Foulkes • St. Louis, Missouri
Judith Fredericks • Folsom, California
Fun House Toy Company • Warrendale, Pennsylvania
Don Glut • Burbank, California
Cliff Green • Provo, Utah
Dennis Grimm • Aurora, Colorado
Mike Howgate • London, England
Greg Holmes • Hutchinson, Kansas
Alfred Iannarelli • Toronto, Canada
Robert Klippel • Denver, Colorado
Rick Koch • Chagrin Falls, Ohio
David Krentz • Valencia, California

Charles McGrady • Gillespie, Illinois
Tony McVey • San Francisco, California
Bob Morales • Colton, California
Jeff Quinn • Vernon, Connecticut
Glenn Ridenour • Warrendale, Pennsylvania
Michael Rusher • Long Beach, California
Steve Schultz • Boulder, Colorado
Riff Smith • Louisville, Kentucky
Space Station • Denver, Colorado
Keith Strasser • Smithtown, New York
Evan Stuart • Longmont, Colorado
Marc Tassone • Rio Rancho, New Mexico
Triceratops Hills Ranch • Englewood, Colorado
Ronald Vasquez • Pueblo, Colorado
Gary Williams • Toronto, Canada

And an extra-special "Thank You" to Dean Walker of Pfafftown, North Carolina. Dean contributed hundreds of photographs for this book, along with a wealth of information and insight. Through his company, DeJankins, Dean buys and sells dinosaur collectibles, and produces a great series of trading cards based on various dinosaur collectibles. He can be reached at (910) 922-1542 from 6 p.m. to 10 p.m. Eastern time. One of the all-time big-time dinosaur collectors, Dean is also one of the nicest people you could ever hope to know!

THE HISTORY OF DINOSAUR FIGURES

Dinosaurs have long fascinated mankind with their enormous size and strange appearance. Were we to somehow go back in time to their strange and seemingly alien world, it would surely be little different than traveling to another planet. Artists, scientists, and dreamers have long and often attempted to determine what dinosaurs looked like, starting back in ancient times when dinosaur fossil discoveries sparked legends of dragons; through the nineteenth century, when the dinosaurs of The Crystal Palace amazed Victorian England onlookers; and on to today's computer-generated dinosaurs in Steven Spielberg's Jurassic Park. Using our imagination to portray the appearance of dinosaurs has been especially popular in the twentieth century, and the end products of those great creative minds have now become very collectible.

Most dinosaur toys and figures were produced starting in the 1950s, but there are a few exceptions. Metal Brontosaurus and Saber-toothed cat figures were sold at the Chicago World's Fair in 1933 and 1934 in celebration of the Messmore and Damon "World A Million Years Ago Pavilion." Also, a company in Oakland produced flexible wooden toys

in the 1920s and 1930s— "manufactured by Twistums Toy Factory." One of the Twistums was a Brontosaurus. This toy is rare, but it does show up at antique toy shows, occasionally commanding several hundred dollars for collectors. A set of lead human figures—four humans and two dinosaurs—was produced in the 1930s for the popular radio program, Og, Son of Fire.

One of the pioneer dinosaur manufacturing companies was Sell Rite Giftware, best known as SRG. Their lead dinosaur figures were given a patina-faux-bronze look (originally marketed as a "Royal Bronze Finish") and some are dated 1947, and earlier, on the belly. Each of the figures came in two sizes, and they are highly desired by collectors today. The small figures were about two or three inches long, and the larger were twice that size. Detail was not very crisp, and the appearance was rather "basic," but baby boomers have fond memories of taking home an SRG dinosaur obtained during one of their museum visits as a child. Many nostalgia buffs seek the complete set today. Along with all of the most popular dinosaurs, SRG figures included a caveman and cavewoman, flying pterosaurs, a mammoth, a mosasaur, and the super-rare Dinicthys—a giant prehistoric fish with large bony jaws. Each included a small card with a picture and information about the animal. Many of the large-version SRGs were reissued in gray-colored plastic in the 1960s, but they are extremely difficult to find today.

Without question, some of the most familiar, well-sculpted, and popular dinosaur figures were produced by the Louis Marx Company in the late 1950s. Like so many artists since, the toy sculptors at Marx based their prehistoric animal designs on the paintings of Charles R. Knight, and upon the Age of Reptiles mural painted by Rudolph Zallinger. In fact, *Life* magazine showed the Zallinger mural art on several front covers during this period, further exposing the art and making it very well known.

At the time, the Marx company was already enjoying success with several boxed playsets full of soldiers, buildings, horses, or vehicles, and the time was right for a prehistoric theme set. The Prehistoric Times playsets came in large boxes with artwork on the lid. The sets consisted of numerous dinosaur and prehistoric animal figures, with cavemen, palm trees, ferns, and rocky groundwork included to allow kids of the late 1950s and early 1960s to use their imagination and travel back millions of years in time. The idea was so popular that Marx produced a dozen different boxed playsets based on a prehistoric theme, and also sold the figures loose in store bins, and packaged in bags and on blister cards. Prehistoric animals were good sellers for Marx in the late 1950s and early 1960s. Besides the soft-plastic playset figures, Marx issued a variety of sizes of hard-plastic dinosaurs, tin metal friction dinosaurs, and figures to be painted.

Eventually, Marx was joined by others in the world of dinosaur toy production. Nabisco Rice Honeys and Wheat Honeys cereals included a one-inch-long dinosaur figure packed free inside specially marked boxes. Kids could consume box after box of cereal to collect all ten figures, or they could send fifty cents to Nabisco and receive not only the complete set, but also a cardboard time wheel that provided a short description of each item. A later promotion by Nabisco included a free prehistoric mammal in each box—eight in all.

The J.H. Miller Company's manufacturing plant in Chicago produced hollow, waxy-plastic dinosaurs and prehistoric animals in two different sizes in the late 1950s. Because these "toys" were so delicate,

many were broken from rough play. Often, they simply melted in the hot sun when left outdoors. Consequently, the Miller figures are tough to come by today, and collectors constantly seek them out. The large figures were over half-a-foot long, and included the most popular dinosaurs as well as a Woolly Rhino and Mastodon. A caveman, cavewoman, and even a cave itself were also made in the hollow wax-like plastic. A Saber-toothed Cat and Pterodactyl are especially difficult Miller figures to find today because they were designed in an especially delicate manner, and nearly always broke when kids hit them together in play.

If the large figures can be considered rare, then the smaller versions of the Miller prehistoric line are nearly impossible to find. Animals in the small line that weren't included in the larger assortment included a Protoceratops, Brontops, and duck-billed Trachodon. Other small Millers were almost identical in design (if not in size) to their larger counterparts: Tyrannosaurus, Stegosaurus, Dimetrodon, Brontosaurus, and Sloth.

At the same time that the Miller, Nabisco, and Marx dinosaurs were so popular in the United States, a company named Chialu was producing

Miller-sized prehistoric animal figures in Italy. The Chialu figures were imported into the U.S., but are harder to find than even the Miller dinosaurs. Chialu figures always sell for more than a hundred dollars today. They are finely painted, and made of a plaster-like composition material with metal wire frames inside. We know about the wire armature because several have been discovered broken. Some figures that make up the set are unidentifiable as any of the prehistoric animals known to science, while others are very well done and quite accurate.

Another Italian company—Orsenigo—produced large- and small-sized dinosaur figures made out of a soft rubbery material. The Orsenigo dinosaurs are considered by some to be rather ugly, but they are nonetheless very collectible, and bring in some fairly high values today.

In England during the 1950s and 1960s, Shredded Wheat cereal boxes contained one of a set of twenty prehistoric animals in an off-white colored hard plastic. The "Shreddies" cereal premiums were as popular with kids in England as the Nabiscos were in America. Two other companies that made soft plastic dinosaur toys in the land of Queen Elizabeth were Timpo Toys and Cherilea. All are highly desired by collectors around the world today.

Yet another dinosaur figure manufacturer of the era whose figures are highly sought after today is Linde. The Linde prehistorics, which came in marbled, green-colored, soft plastic, were only a couple of inches long. They were coffee premiums in the late 1950s. The eight figures are based on the Zallinger mural. The Rhamphorhynchus figure is the most valuable today. Other dinosaurs from the same era that are eminently collectible today include the many ceramic prehistorics from Japan—especially those from a company called Abbeon—and the metal figures produced by Alva.

Other companies tried to reap their share of the dinosaur toy market around the mid-point of the century by producing tiny dinosaur figures in bright colors. Both Timmee Toys and Ajax manufactured soft plastic dinosaur toys of their own design in reds, greens, yellows, etc., packaged in clear bags with attractive header cards designed to grab the attention of kids. Where Marx generally offered their dinosaur figures in earth tones, such as green, brown, and gray, other firms' brightly colored dinosaurs also sold well in the dino heyday of the late 1950s and early 1960s.

MPC sold thousands of brightly colored dinosaur toy figures in soft plastic, most of which were based upon the earlier designs of Louis Marx. MPC did create a Brontosaurus of its own design, along with a set of other prehistoric animals unique to MPC. The Machrauchenia, Dire Wolf, Ceratogaulus, Diatryma, and Glyptodon are a cut above the other MPC prehistorics in realism, and are thought to have been created by the same people responsible for the beautiful Marx figures. MPC packaged their dinosaurs in bags, blister cards, and playsets, in the tried and true tradition of Marx.

The dinosaur craze experienced a cooling off period during the second half of the 1960s. Best Plastics manufactured flat, soft plastic prehistorics sold with candy at this time, and Winneco copied the MPC figures (which had already copied those made by Marx). Marx reissued some of their prehistoric playsets in the 1970s, but the finest prehistorics of that decade again came from England. Invicta Plastics manufactured a beautiful line of soft plastic prehistoric animal figures in conjunction with the British Museum, in London. The unpainted figures were highly detailed, and based upon recent scientific discoveries. Many of the prehistoric animals Invicta depicted had never been made as toy figures before. The line was sold widely in the U.S., as well as in other countries. The final two figures in the series came out in 1993—beautifully crafted Dimetrodon and Lambeosaurus representations.

Another interesting museum line of unpainted soft plastic prehistoric animals came out of the Royal Ontario Museum, in Toronto, Canada. The ROMs, as they were called, were generally smaller than those of the British Museum, and they represented prehistoric animals known to have lived in what is today Canada. The eight figures were cast only in gray and green plastic, but Hong Kong-made copies of several of the figures came in red, orange, yellow, and tan. Fred Kay was the sculptor of the ROM dinosaurs.

Starlux, a French toy manufacturer, still produces figures in hand-painted hard plastic. Their prehistoric line is quite extensive, and includes many prehistoric mammals, humans, dinosaurs, and other ancient creatures that no other company has ever offered. The firm has offered the series for over twenty years, and does so to this day, although a number of the toys were recently discontinued.

In the 1980s, many dinosaur toys became action figures. Such toy lines as Bone Age, Playskool's Definitely Dinosaurs, and Tyco's Dino Riders included both dinosaur and human figures that youngsters could ride on. All included accessories and were articulated for movement. Probably the most collectible of the Definitely Dinosaurs line was the huge Ultrasaurus.

Mego produced a line of dinosaurs and cavepeople called "One Million Years B.C." that included a Tyrannosaurus, a Dimetrodon, and a Woolly Rhino

figure, all of which are very rare today.

H-G Toys were manufactured in the Asian market, but sold in America. This line included large hard-plastic dinosaurs with moveable limbs and working mouths, plus rubbery-plastic smaller cavemen and prehistoric animals. They all have a unique appearance that some collectors are just beginning to appreciate and seek.

The action figure idea continued into the 1990s with the huge Sky Kids-Thunderbeasts line. Each poseable dinosaur included a real dino bone fossil with a certificate of authenticity. A set of smaller-sized dinosaurs was released a few years later.

Many collectors seek the Topps small dinosaur figures that were included with bags of candy in 1988. The three-inch figures were soft plastic in colors of brown, gray, and green. Topps subsequently released a set of soft plastic dinosaurs in 1993, for the movie *Jurassic Park*. Following much the same idea as the one behind the British Museum dinosaurs, Safari Ltd. began producing prehistoric animal figures that were manufactured in a rubbery plastic and came completely painted. The figures are made under the guidance of the Carnegie Museum, in Pittsburgh. Carnegie/Safari continues to add new figures to the line, retire old ones, and update (enhance the accuracy of) existing dinosaurs to this date. The Carnegie figures proved so popular that the British Museum/Invicta company began painting their line for awhile just to keep up. Most of the Carnegie figures were sculpted by Forest Rogers.

Dinosaurs cast in beautiful pewter metals were popular in the 1980s, and they have continued to retain their popularity. Companies such as Ral Partha, Rawcliffe, Spoontiques, Wade Miller, and others are actively sought by collectors today since they are no longer manufactured. The Wade Miller figures out of Utah, in particular, were regarded as being scientifically accurate to a large degree.

One feature that tends to distinguish 1990s dinosaur figures from those produced during the 1950s and 1960s is the absence of a dragging tail. Scientists recognized that of the many dinosaur footprint trails known to exist, none ever showed evidence of a dragging tail. It is now widely believed that dinosaurs held their tails high off the ground, and the latest toys and figures are beginning to reflect this refinement. Some of the most scientifically accurate dinosaur toy figures on today's market are produced by Battat. These figures are associated with the Boston Museum of Science. Three sets have been produced, and it is hoped that more will follow. Sculpted by Dan LoRusso and Greg Wenzel, the dinosaurs are made of soft, rubbery plastic, and are completely painted. These beautiful figures are, hopefully, the way of the future—a future in which sculptors use the latest scientific data to create the most accurate possible dinosaur representations. Nevertheless, there will always be collectors like myself who hold a special fondness for the look, however fanciful, of the toy dinosaurs from our own youth.

—**Mike Fredericks**

Fig. 1-1: Yellow Dimetrodon

Fig. 1-2: Stegosaurus

PLASTIC AND VINYL
FIGURES

Fig. 1-3: Triceratops

AAA
Large painted soft vinyl figures, marked with three "*As*" in a circle and "made in China"

Dimetrodon, yellow with red fin base, 17"
   long (fig. 1-1) $10-15
Dromaeosaurus, with big toes, 10" tall . . . 10-15
Parasaurolophus, 12" tall 10-15
Stegosaurus, slender body style, 16" long
   (fig. 1-2) 10-15
Triceratops, green, 14" long (fig. 1-3) 10-15

Fig. 1-4: Assortment of boxed, hard-plastic, painted Ajax figures from Hong Kong

AJAX
**Miniature plastic dinosaurs, 2",
1950s-1960s (fig. 1-4)**

Brontosaurus, soft colored plastic $3-5
Brontosaurus, hard painted plastic, boxed,
   1960s (fig. 1-5) 10-15
Dimetrodon, soft colored plastic 3-5
Dimetrodon, hard painted plastic, boxed,
   1960s 10-15
Parasaurolophus, soft colored plastic
   (fig. 1-6) 3-5
Parasaurolophus, hard painted plastic,
   boxed, 1960s 10-15
Plateosaurus, soft colored plastic 3-5
Plateosaurus, hard painted plastic, boxed,
   1960s (fig. 1-7) 10-15
Pterodactyl, soft colored plastic (fig. 1-8) . . . 3-5
Pterodactyl, hard painted plastic, boxed,
   1960s 10-15
Stegosaurus, soft colored plastic 3-5
Stegosaurus, hard painted plastic, boxed,
   1960s (fig. 1-9) 10-15
Triceratops, soft colored plastic 3-5
Triceratops, hard painted plastic, boxed,
   1960s (fig. 1-10) 10-15
Tyrannosaurus, soft colored plastic 3-5
Tyrannosaurus, hard painted plastic,
   boxed, 1960s 10-15

Fig. 1-5: Hard painted plastic Brontosaurus

Fig. 1-8: Soft colored plastic Pterodactyl

Fig. 1-6: Soft colored plastic Parasaur-olophus

Fig. 1-7: Hard painted plastic Plateosaurus

Fig. 1-9: Hard painted plastic Stegosaurus

BEST
Thin plastic, 3" long, most are green, originally packaged in "Monster Grab Bag" with toy, candy, and dinosaur, 1960s

(Note: Prices are for dinosaurs only. Full packages are worth $10-15.)

Ankylosaurus $4-6
Brontosaurus 4-6
Caveman with rock 4-6
Caveman with club 4-6
Dimetrodon 4-6
Iguanodon 4-6
Megatherium (fig. 1-11) 4-6
Parasaurolophus 4-6
Rhamphorhynchus (fig. 1-12) 4-6
Sabertooth Cat 4-6
Stegosaurus 4-6
Struthiomimus 4-6
Trachodon 4-6
Triceratops 4-6
Tyrannosaurus Rex 4-6
Woolly Mammoth 4-6

Fig. 1-10: Hard painted plastic Triceratops

BOLEY
Vinyl dinosaurs, made in China, sold at Woolworth's, 1990s

Apatosaurus, 5.5" (fig. 1-13) $1-3
Brachiosaurus, 5.5" 1-3
Dimetrodon, 5.5" (fig. 1-14) 1-3
Iguanodon, 5.5" (fig. 1-15) 1-3

Fig. 1-11: Megatherium

Fig. 1-13: Apatosaurus

Fig. 1-15: Iguanodon

Fig. 1-12: Rhamphorhynchus

Fig. 1-14: Dimetrodon

Pachycephalosaurus, 5.5" $1-3
Pteranodon, 5.5" 1-3
Pteranodon, 9" 1-3
Triceratops, 9" 1-3
Tyrannosaurus Rex, 9" 1-3
Utahraptor, 9" 1-3
Velociraptor Pair, 5.5" 1-3
Set of twelve 4" dinosaurs 15-20

Hatchling Series
Brachiosaurus with hatchling $5-8
Dimetrodon with hatchling 5-8
Parasaurolophus with hatchling 5-8
Stegosaurus with hatchling 5-8
Triceratops with hatchling 5-8
Tyrannosaurus with hatchling 5-8

Boley Evolution Series
Apatosaurus with egg, dinosaur, and bones .$4-6
Parasaurolophus with egg, dinosaur, and bones
    4-6
Pteranodon with egg, dinosaur, and bones . . 4-6
Stegosaurus with egg, dinosaur, and bones . 4-6
Triceratops with egg, dinosaur, and bones . . 4-6
Tyrannosaurus with egg, dinosaur, and bones 4-6

Jurassic Dinosaur Two-Packs
Stegosaurus and Parasaurolophus (fig. 1-16)$2-4
Triceratops and Tyrannosaurus (fig. 1-17) . . 2-4

Fig. 1-16: Stegosaurus and Parasaurolophus

Fig. 1-17: Triceratops and Tyrannosaurus

BONE AGE
Action figures, Kenner, 1988

Anklor (fig. 1-18) $4-8
Brontus (fig. 1-19) 4-8
Codus 4-8
Deitron (fig. 1-20) 4-8
Dynacus (fig. 1-21) 4-8
Plesior 4-8
Ptero 4-8
Stegus 4-8
Tritops 4-8
T-Rex 4-8

Burger King Figures
Dimetrodon $2-3
Mammoth (fig. 1-22) 2-3
Smilodon (fig. 1-23) 2-3
T-Rex 2-3

Cavemen and Accessories
Ice Clan, Mok (fig. 1-24) $2-4
Ice Clan, Nord 2-4
Ice Clan, Tund the Thunderous 2-4
Lava Clan, Bull 2-4

Lava Clan, Karn (fig. 1-25) $2-4
Lava Clan, Volc the Voracious 2-4
Stone Clan, Crag the Clubber (fig. 1-26) 2-4
Stone Clan, Kos 2-4
Weapon, Club Flinger (fig. 1-27) 4-7
Weapon, Hammer Hook 4-7
Weapon, Ram Bammer 4-7

BOSTON MUSEUM OF SCIENCE DINOSAUR COLLECTION
1/40 scale painted PVC plastic, sculpted by Dan LoRusso and Greg Wenzel of The Dinosaur Studio, Battat, 1990s

Acrocanthosaurus, 1997 . . . . $5-10
Amargasaurus, with finned back, 1996 . . . 5-10
Carnotaurus, 1997 5-10
Ceratosaurus, 1996 5-10
Dilophosaurus, foot raised, 1995 5-10
Diplodocus, rearing, 1995 (fig. 1-28) 20-25
Edmontonia, armored short dinosaur, 1996 8-12
Euoplocephalous, 1997 5-10
Gallimimus, running, 1995 5-10
Maiasaura, 1997 5-10
Ouranosaurus, spotted and finned, 1996 . . 5-10

Fig. 1-18: Anklor

Fig. 1-19: Brontus

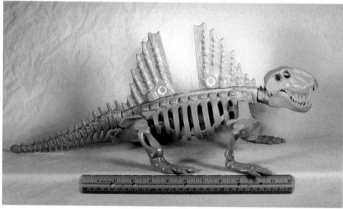

Fig. 1-20: Deitron

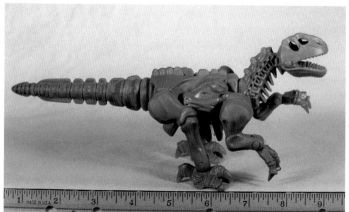

Fig. 1-21: Dynacus

Fig. 1-22: Mammoth

Fig. 1-23: Smilodon

Fig. 1-24: Ice Clan, Mok

Fig. 1-25: Lava Clan, Karn

Fig. 1-26: Stone Clan, Crag the Clubber

Fig. 1-27: Weapon, Club Flinger

Fig. 1-28: Diplodocus, rearing

Fig. 1-29: Diplodocus

Fig. 1-30: Iguandon   **Fig. 1-31:** Megalosaurus

Pachycephalosaurus, 1997 . . . . $5-10
Parasaurolophus, 1997 5-10
Stegosaurus, striped with long legs, 1995 . . 5-10
Styracosaurus, striped with two-toned horns,
    1996 5-10
Triceratops, goring position, 1995 5-10
Tyrannosaurus, striped, 1995 8-12
Utahraptor, spotted with big claws, 1996 . . 5-10

BRITISH MUSEUM OF NATURAL HISTORY
1/45 scale, Invicta Plastics, 1970s-1990s

Fig. 1-32: Pteranodon

Apatosaurus, light gray, 18" long, 1980s $10-15
Baryonyx, 9.5" long, 1990 10-15
Blue Whale, first of series, 1973 5-8
Brachiosaurus, greenish gray, 11", 1984 . 20-25
Cetiosaurus, purple sauropod, 13" long . . . 8-12
Dimetrodon, brown, 3", UK exclusive,
    not painted, 1993 15-20
Diplodocus, dark gray, 22" long, 1974
(fig. 1-29) 12-18
Glyptodont, tan, 3" long, 1975 4-7
Ichthyosaurus, blue, 6" long, 1986 7-12
Iguanodon, yellow, 7.25", 1980 (fig. 1-30) . . . 5-8
Lambeosaurus, 7.5" long, UK exclusive, not
    painted, 1993 15-20

Mamenchisaurus (long-necked sauropod),
    cream-colored, 10.5", 1988 . . . . $9-14
Megalosaurus, green, 5" tall, 1974 (fig. 1-31) 5-8
Muttaburrasaurus, light brown, 6" long,
    1980s 5-8
Plesiosaur, blue, 11" long, 1978 7-12
Pliosaur, green, 8.5" long 4-7
Pteranodon, tan plastic, 6" wingspan, 1978
    (fig. 1-32) 4-7
Scelidosaurus, brown, 3.5" long, 1975 4-7
Stegosaurus, pink, 5", 1975 5-8
Stenonychosaurus (Troodon), cream-colored
    on base, 5", pulled pending litigation,
    1988 20-25
Triceratops, brown, 6" long, 1975 5-8
Tyrannosaurus, burgundy, 10.5" long, 1975 6-10
Woolly Mammoth, brown, 5" long, 1975 . . . 6-10

BULLYLAND
German vinyl figures, 1990s

*Large Dinosaurs (Standard Size),
average 3.5" long*

Ankylosaurus (fig. 1-33) $3-5
Brontosaurus 3-5
Cave Bear, 1996 addition, discontinued 4-8
Dimetrodon (fig. 1-34) 3-5
Elasmosaurus 3-5
Neanderthal . . . . .not released
Pteranodon (fig. 1-35) 3-5
Stegosaurus 3-5
Triceratops 3-5
Tyrannosaurus 3-5
Velociraptor, 1996 addition, discontinued . . . 4-8
Woolly Mammoth, 1996 addition,
    discontinued (fig. 1-36) 4-8

Fig. 1-33: Ankylosaurus **Fig. 1-34:** Dimetrodon

Fig. 1-35: Pteranodon

Fig. 1-36: Woolly Mammoth

*Medium Dinosaurs, painted vinyl, average 3", mold-
ed-on base, currently available*

Apatosaurus $2-4
Brachiosaurus 2-4
Dimetrodon 2-4
Dilophosaurus 2-4
Elasmosaurus 2-4
Parasaurolophus 2-4
Pteranodon 2-4
Spinosaurus 2-4
Stegosaurus leaning on tree 2-4
Triceratops 2-4
Tyrannosaurus 2-4
Velociraptor 2-4

*Minis, sold as figures, pencil topper,
and key chains, 2", 1991*

Ankylosaurus . . . . 50¢-$1.00
Apatosaurus (fig. 1-37) . . . . 50¢-1.00
Dimetrodon (fig. 1-38) . . . . 50¢-1.00
Pteranodon . . . . 50¢-1.00
Stegosaurus (fig. 1-39) . . . . 50¢-1.00
Triceratops . . . . 50¢-1.00
Tyrannosaurus . . . . 50¢-1.00

Fig. 1-37: Apatosaurus **Fig. 1-38:** Dimetrodon

Fig. 1-39: Stegosaurus

Figs. 1-40 and 1-41: Brontosaurus

*Painted/Unpainted soft vinyl series, average 3",
1991, discontinued*

Brontosaurus, solid color or painted, 1991
   (figs. 1-40 and 1-41) $1-2
Dimetrodon, solid color or painted, 1991 . . . 1-2
Elasmosaurus, solid color or painted, 1991 . 1-2
Pteranodon (tripod position), solid color or
   painted, 1991 (figs. 1-42 and 1-43) 1-2
Stegosaurus, solid color or painted, 1991
   (figs. 1-44 and 1-45) 1-2
Triceratops, solid color or painted 1991 1-2
Tyrannosaurus, solid color or painted, 1991 . 1-2

Figs. 1-42 and 1-43: Pteranodon

Figs. 1-44 and 1-45: Stegosaurus

Fig. 1-46: Anchitherium

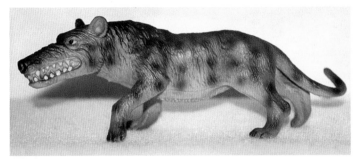

Fig. 1-47: Andrewsarchus

Fig. 1-48:
Cave Bear

Fig. 1-49: Coelodonta

Fig. 1-50: Diatryma

Fig. 1-51: Megatherium

Prehistoric Time—People and Animals

Anchitherium, ancient horse, 4" long
(fig. 1-46) $6-10
Andrewsaurchus, brown, 7" long
(fig. 1-47) 10-15
Cave Bear, 4" long, brown (fig. 1-48) 5-8
Chalicotherium, claw animal, yellow,
5" long 10-15
Coelodonta, Woolly Rhino, 3.5" (fig. 1-49) . 10-15
Deinotherium, tusk elephant, 4.5" 15-20
Diatryma, giant ratite, gray, 4" (fig. 1-50) . . 7-10
Eusmilus, saber-toothed cat, 4" 6-10
Megaloceros Giganteus, giant deer, 5" 7-10
Mammoth, gray with long tusks, 4" long . . 15-20
Megatherium, giant ground sloth, 6.5"
(fig. 1-51) 15-20

Cave People

Australopithicus, anatomically correct male,
late addition $5-8
Neanderthal gatherer, 2.5" 5-8
Neanderthal hunter, 2" 5-8
Neanderthal shaman, 2.5" 5-8
Neanderthal woman, 2" 5-8
Campfire 5-8

Prehistoric Disney Series, European only, no U.S. distribution, 1990s

Caveman Mickey Mouse $5-10
Cavewoman Minnie Mouse 5-10
Donald Duck and Brontosaurus 5-10
Mickey and Brontosaurus 5-10
Pluto and Triceratops 5-10

World of Dinosaurs, Museum Line, currently available

Allosaurus, green with stripes, 1/25 scale,
    5" (fig. 1-52) $7-10
Apatosaurus, blue-gray, 12" long
    (fig. 1-53) 15-20
Brachiosaurus, green, 1/40 scale, 9" tall . 15-20
Dilophosaurus, green with red crest, 1:20
    scale, 8" long (fig. 1-54) 8-12
Dimetrodon, olive with brown sail back,
    5" long (fig. 1-55) 7-10
Parasaurolophus, green and black striped
    with yellow belly, 1/30 scale (fig. 1-56) . . 8-12
Pteranodon, brown with wings spread,
8" long (fig. 1-57) 8-12
Stegosaurus, brown with reddish spines,
    4" long 7-10

Fig. 1-54: Dilophosaurus

Fig. 1-55: Dimetrodon

Fig. 1-52: Allosaurus

Fig. 1-56: Parasaurolophus

Fig. 1-53: Apatosaurus

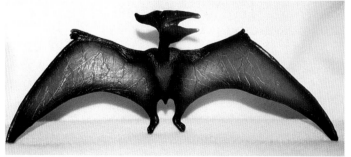

Fig. 1-57: Pteranodon

Fig. 1-58: Triceratops

Fig. 1-59: Velociraptor

Fig. 1-60: Cadillacs & Dinosaurs

Triceratops, orange-ish, 5" long (fig. 1-58) . $8-12
Tyrannosaurus, rust-colored with black
    stripes, 10" long 8-12
Velociraptor, striped, 1/20 scale, 5"
    (fig. 1-59) 8-12

Glow-in-the-Dark versions of Museum Line,
discontinued

Allosaurus, 1/25 scale, 5" $10-15
Apatosaurus, 12" long 20-25
Brachiosaurus, 1/40 scale, 9" tall 20-25
Dilophosaurus, 1/20 scale, 8" long 15-20
Dimetrodon, 5" long 10-15
Parasaurolophus, 1/30 scale 15-20
Pteranodon, 8" long 15-20
Stegosaurus, 4" long 10-15
Triceratops, 5" long 15-20
Tyrannosaurus, 10" long 15-20
Velociraptor, 1/20 scale, 5" 15-20

Dinosaur Puzzles series

Apatosaurus skeleton in egg $5-10
Stegosaurus skeleton in egg 5-10
Tyrannosaurus skeleton in egg 5-10

CADILLACS & DINOSAURS
(Dino-Riders re-issues), Tyco, 1993-1994

Hammer Terhune, Tyco $5-7
Hannah Dundee, Tyco 20-25
Hermes, Tyco 6-10
Jack "Cadillac" Tenrec, Tyco 6-10
Junge Fighting Jack Tenrec, Tyco 6-10
Kentrosaurus, Tyco (fig. 1-60, top) 10-15
Mustapha Cairo, Tyco 6-10
Snake Eyes, Tyco 6-10
Triceratops, Tyco (fig. 1-60, bottom) . . . 10-15
Vehicle, Hammer's Tribike, Tyco 10-15
Vehicle, Jack's Cadillac, Tyco 25-30
Vehicle, Jack's Glider, Tyco 10-15
Vice Terhune, Tyco 6-10
Zeke, Tyco 6-10

Fig. 1-61: Gigantosaurus

Fig. 1-62: Stegosaurus

Fig. 1-63: Styracosaurus

Fig. 1-64: Triceratops

Fig. 1-65: Tyrannosaurus

CARNAGE SERIES
Brightly painted action figures, Resaurus, 1998

Gigantosaurus, with labeled base, 14"
   long (fig. 1-61) $13-18
Stegosaurus, 11" (fig. 1-62) 13-18
Styracosaurus, 10" long (fig. 1-63) 13-18
Triceratops, 10" (fig. 1-64) 13-18
Tyrannosaurus, with base, 13" long
   (fig. 1-65) 13-18
Velociraptor, with base, 12" long
   (fig. 1-66) 13-18

Fig. 1-66: Velociraptor

Fig. 1-67: Carnegie Safari Ltd. painted vinyl figures

Fig. 1-68: Allosaurus

CARNEGIE SAFARI LTD.
Carnegie Museum of Natural History, Pittsburgh, painted vinyl figures, 1/40 scale, 1988-present
(fig. 1-67)

Allosaurus, green wavy paint pattern,
  9" long, 1988 (fig. 1-68) $6-10
Apatosaurus adult, 22" long, 1988 18-25
Apatosaurus baby, 6.5" long, 1988 4-8
Baryonyx, 9" long, 1998 (fig. 1-69) 5-9
Brachiosaurus, foot forward,
  22" tall, 1988 20-30
Carnotaurus, 6" long, 1997 (fig. 1-70) 4-8
Corythosaurus, 8" long, 1993 6-10
Deinonychus trio, 1990, discontinued
  in 1997 7-12

Fig. 1-72: Kronosaurus

Deinosuchus, 8.5" long, 1996 . . . . $7-12
Deltadromeus Agilis, 5" long, 1998 4-8
Dilophosaurus pair, 4" long, 1994 7-12
Dimetrodon, 1988, discontinued in 1997
  fig. 1-71) 5-10
Diplodocus, yellow, 24" long, 1988 20-30
Elasmosaurus, 10.5" long, 1991 8-12
Euoplocephalus, armored dinosaur, green,
  1988, discontinued in 1997 8-12
Iguanodon, gray with white/brown spots,
  6" tall, 1992 7-10
Kronosaurus, 13" long, 1997 (fig. 1-72) . . 12-16
Maiasaura and nest, 8" long, 1996 12-18
Mosasaurus, 6" long, 1991 6-10
Pachycephalosaurus, head butter,
  on base, 7" long, 1990 (fig. 1-73) 6-10
Parasaurolophus, green striped with yellow,
  5" tall, 1988 (fig. 1-74) 5-8
Plateosaurus, 7.5" long, 1995 6-10

Fig. 1-69: Baryonyx

Fig. 1-70: Carnotaurus

Fig. 1-73: Pachycephalosaurus

Fig. 1-71: Dimetrodon

Fig. 1-74: Parasaurolophus

Fig. 1-75: Protoceratops with eggs

Fig. 1-76: Saltasaurus

Fig. 1-77: Spinosaurus

Protoceratops with eggs, yellow painted
  vinyl, 3.25" long, 1988 (fig. 1-75) $8-12
Pteranodon, 4.5" long, 1988 3-5
Quetzalcoatlus, 7" across, 1998 5-9
Saltosaurus, 11.5" long, 1997 (fig. 1-76) . . . 6-10
Smilodon, 1988, discontinued in 1997 8-12
Spinosaurus, 9", 1992 (fig. 1-77) 8-12
Stegosaurus, tan and brown mottled,
  6" long, 1988 (fig. 1-78) 6-10
Stegosaurus, yellow with brown back,
  6" long, 1988, discontinued 8-12
Triceratops, 7" long, 1988 6-10
Tyrannosaurus, green with pink mouth,
  yellow eyes, 11" long, 1988 7-10

Fig. 1-78: Stegosaurus

CHERILEA
Series of 6 soft plastic painted figures, England, 1950s

Dimetrodon, 3" long (fig. 1-79) $20-30
Diplodocus 20-30
Pteranodon 20-30
Stegosaurus 20-30
Triceratops, 3" long (fig. 1-80) 20-30
Tyrannosaurus 20-30

Fig. 1-79: Dimetrodon   **Fig. 1-80:** Triceratops

DINOLAND SERIES
Kaiyodo, 1980s-1990s

Allosaurus, brown in gold 6" x 4" box,
  American Museum of Natural History
  (fig. 1-81) $12-20
Allosaurus, red and black in white box
  with map background (fig. 1-82) 15-25
Camarasaurus, gray in window box
  with map background (fig. 1-83) 15-25
Dimetrodon, box is 6" x 4", American
  Museum of Natural History (fig. 1-84) . . 12-20
Elasmosaurus, green in white box with
  map background (fig. 1-85) 15-25
Lambeosaurus, yellow and brown in white
  box with map background (fig. 1-86) . . 15-25
Mosasaurus, box is 6" x 4", American
  Museum of Natural History (fig. 1-87) . . 12-20

Fig. 1-81: Allosaurus

Fig. 1-82: Allosaurus

Fig. 1-83: Camarasaurus

Fig. 1-88: Stegosaurus

Fig. 1-84: Dimetrodon

Fig. 1-85: Elasmosaurus

Fig. 1-89: Triceratops

Fig. 1-86: Lambeosaurus

Fig. 1-87: Mosasaurus

Stegosaurus, brown in white box with
  map background (fig. 1-88) $15-25
Triceratops, gray in white box with
  map background (fig. 1-89) 15-25
Velociraptor, box is 6" x 4", American
  Museum of Natural History (fig. 1-90) . . 12-20

Fig. 1-90: Velociraptor

DINOSAURS BUSTERS
Colorful plastic figures, MCT, 1993

Ankylosaurus, brown $2-4
Apatosaurus, green 2-4
Dimetrodon, pink, mouth open 2-4
Stegosaurus, violet and red with
  black spots 2-4
Triceratops, blue and violet 2-4
Tyrannosaurus, orange 2-4

Fig. 1-91: Dinosaurs Busters

Fig. 1-92: Spike, Triceratops, 5", Series 2

Fig. 1-93: Ankylosaurus

Fig. 1-94: Brontosaurus

Fig. 1-95: Cave Bear

Fig. 1-96: Caveman

EXTREME DINOSAURS
Mattel, 1997

Bad Rap, Velociraptor, 5", Series,
  3—Dino Vision, Mattel, 1997 . . . . $5-10
Bullzeye, Pteranodon, 5", Series 1,
  with Extreme Sticker, Mattel, 1997 10-20
Bullzeye, Pteranodon, 5", Series 2,
  Mattel, 1997 5-10
Bullzeye, 5", Series 3, Dino Vision,
  Mattel, 1997 5-10
Hard Rock, 5", Series 3 Dino Vision,
  Mattel, 1997 5-10
Haxx, 5", Series 1, with Extreme Sticker,
  Mattel, 1997 15-30
Haxx, 5", Series 2, Mattel, 1997 5-10
Mega T-Bone, large figure, Mattel, 1997 . . 15-30
Spike, Triceratops, 5", Series 1, with
  Extreme Sticker, Mattel, 1997 10-20
Spike, Triceratops, 5", Series 2,
  Mattel, 1997 (fig. 1-92) 5-10
Spike, Triceratops, 5", Series 3, Dino
  Vision, Mattel, 1997 5-10
Stegz, Stegosaurus, 5", Series 1, with
  Extreme Sticker, Mattel, 1997 10-20
Stegz, Stegosaurus, 5", Series 2, Mattel,
  1997 6-12
T-Bone, T-Rex, 5", Series 1, with Extreme
  Sticker, Mattel, 1997 10-20

T-Bone, T-Rex, 5", Series 2, Mattel, 1997 . $5-10
T-Bone, T-Rex, 5", Series, 3 Dino Vision,
  Mattel, 1997 5-10
Vehicle, Dino Chopper with T-Bone,
  Mattel, 1997 8-12

DINOSAUR WARRIOR
Plastic figures, large ones articulated,
HG Toys, 1980s

Note: Unless noted, prices are for loose figures.
Ankylosaurus, orange, 3.5" (fig. 1-93) $2-4
Brontosaurus, dark blue plastic, knob
  on head, 9.5" long 10-15
Brontosaurus, dark blue, 4" long (fig. 1-94) . 2-4
Cave Bear, brown with white belly, knob
  on head, 8" tall (fig. 1-95) 10-15

Fig. 1-97: Dimetrodon

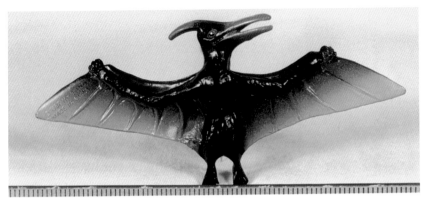

Fig. 1-98: Pteranodon

Fig. 1-102: Woolly Mammoth

Fig. 1-99: Saber-Toothed Tiger

Fig. 1-103: Miniature Collector Pack

Fig. 1-100: Stegosaurus

Fig. 1-101: Triceratops

Caveman, several styles, one piece, each
(fig. 1-96) $2-4
Dimetrodon, 4" long (fig. 1-97) 2-4
Pteranodon, green and yellow, 5" across
(fig. 1-98) 2-4
Saber-Toothed Tiger, knob on head,
7.5" long (fig. 1-99) 10-15
Stegosaurus, orange and black, knob
on head, 11.5" long (fig. 1-100) 10-15
Stegosaurus, orange with white tail spikes,
3.5" long 2-4
Triceratops, green plastic, red eye, knob on
head, 10.5" long 2-4
Triceratops, gray with blue eye, 3.5" long
(fig. 1-101) 2-4
T-Rex, gray with articulated mouth, knob
on back of head, 8" tall 10-15
T-Rex, 3.5" tall 2-4
Woolly Mammoth, brown with white tusks,
eyeliner, 8" long (fig. 1-102) 10-15
Miniature Collector Pack with 3 dinos,
caveman, rock, and tree (fig. 1-103) 20-30
Dinosaur Mountain Playset, with 4 large
dinosaurs, 3 cavemen, dino life chart . . 40-60

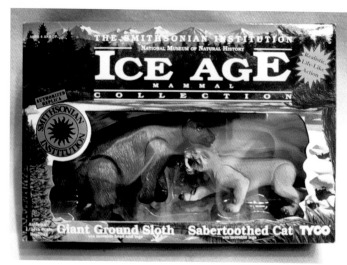

Fig. 1-104: Giant Ground Sloth
and Saber-Toothed Cat

Fig. 1-105: Allosaurus

Fig. 1-106: Dimetrodon

ICE AGE
Smithsonian Institution series of articulated plastic figures in window boxes, Tyco

Giant Ground Sloth and Saber-Toothed Cat
   (fig. 1-104) $10-20
Woolly Mammoth 10-20

INPRO
Hard plastic painted figures, England, 1972

Allosaurus (fig. 1-105) $4-7
Ankylosaurus 4-7
Brontosaurus, 6", rare 20-30
Corythosaurus 4-7
Dimetrodon (fig. 1-106) 4-7
Heterodontosaurus 4-7
Protoceratops 4-7
Saber-Toothed Tiger (fig. 1-107) 4-7
Saltoposuchus 15-25
Stegosaurus 4-7
Styracosaurus (fig. 1-108) 4-7
Trachodon, only unmarked piece
   in the series 15-25
Triceratops (fig. 1-109) 4-7
Tyrannosaurus 4-7
Woolly Mammoth (fig. 1-110) 4-7
Chiver's Jelly, England, Age of Dinosaurs
   mail order set, 6 figures
   on cardboard, 1977 60-75
Inpro re-issues, "Dinocrats" in softer plastic,
   still available, each 1-2

Fig. 1-107: Saber-Toothed Tiger

Fig. 1-108: Styracosaurus

Fig. 1-109: Triceratops

Fig. 1-110: Woolly Mammoth

Fig. 1-111: Ankylosaurus

Fig. 1-112: Apatosaurus

Fig. 1-113: Brachiosaurus

Fig. 1-114: Dimetrodon

Fig. 1-115: Pachycephalo-saurus

Fig. 1-116: Parasaurolophus

Fig. 1-117: Pteranodon

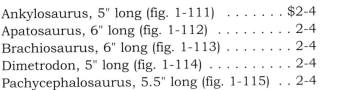

JURASSIC AGE DINOSAUR SKELETON COLLECTION
Funrise, 1990s

Ankylosaurus, 5" long (fig. 1-111) $2-4
Apatosaurus, 6" long (fig. 1-112) 2-4
Brachiosaurus, 6" long (fig. 1-113) 2-4
Dimetrodon, 5" long (fig. 1-114) 2-4
Pachycephalosaurus, 5.5" long (fig. 1-115) . . 2-4
Parasaurolophus, 5" long (fig. 1-116) 2-4
Pteranodon, 5.5" across (fig. 1-117) 2-4
Stegosaurus, 5" long (fig. 1-118) 2-4
Triceratops, 5" long (fig. 1-119) 2-4
Tyrannosaurus, 5" long (fig. 1-120) 2-4

Fig. 1-118: Stegosaurus

Fig. 1-119: Triceratops

Fig. 1-120: Tyrannosaurus

Fig. 1-121: Ankylosaurus

Fig. 1-122: Diplodocus

Fig. 1-123: Elasmosaurus

Fig. 1-124: Iguanodon

Ankylosaurus, green and gray painted vinyl,
4" long, labeled on stomach (fig. 1-121) . $3-5
Apatosaurus 3-5
Brachiosaurus 3-5
Diplodocus (fig. 1-122) 3-5
Elasmosaurus (fig. 1-123) 3-5
Iguanodon, black and green with yellow, 6",
labeled on stomach (fig. 1-124) 3-5
Parasaurolophus 3-5
Stegosaurus, brown and tan with green
eyes, 5" (fig. 1-125) 3-5
Styracosaurus, green-striped, blunt
body style, 4" (fig. 1-126) 3-5
Triceratops (fig. 1-127) 3-5
Tyrannosaurus 3-5

Fig. 1-125: Stegosaurus

Fig. 1-126: Styracosaurus

Fig. 1-127: Triceratops

Fig. 1-128

LINDE COFFEE PREMIUMS
**Olive-colored marbled plastic, 1-2",
Austria, 1950s (fig. 1-128)**

Ankylosaurus (fig. 1-129) $15-25
Brontosaurus 15-25
Dimetrodon (fig. 1-130) 15-25
Rhamphorhynchus, flying reptile, rare . . . 60-80
Sphenecodon (fig. 1-131) 15-25
Stegosaurus 15-25
Triceratops 15-25
Tyrannosaurus 15-25

Fig. 1-129: Ankylosaurus   **Fig. 1-130:** Dimetrodon

Fig. 1-131: Sphenecodon

MAROLIN/VEB PLAHO
**Plastic figures from Germany, 1967-1990s
(fig. 1-132)**

Note: In 1967 an East German firm, VEB Plaho, a division of Marolin, released a series of dinosaur figures through the Phyletic Museum of Sena in Thuringia, Germany. It is believed that the figures may have been reduced versions of molds acquired from a buyout of an older European firm. The figures were sold in the Museum until the mid-1980s. In June 1990, they were re-released under the name Marolin.

Brontosaurus, 5.5" long, VEB Plaho,
   1960s-1980s $15-25
Brontosaurus, 5.5" long, Marolin, 1990s
   (fig. 1-133) 10-15
Iguanodon, 4" tall, VEB Plaho,
   1960s-1980s 15-25
Iguanodon, 4" tall, Marolin, 1990s 10-15
Mammoth, 5" long, VEB Plaho,
   1960s-1980s 15-25

Fig. 1-132

Fig. 1-133: Brontosaurus

Fig. 1-134: Mammoth

Fig. 1-135: Monoclonius

Fig. 1-136: Pteranodon

Mammoth, 5" long, Marolin, 1990s
(fig. 1-134) $10-15
Megatherium, 3.5" tall, VEB Plaho,
1960s-1980s 15-25
Megatherium, 3.5" tall, Marolin, 1990s . . . 10-15
Monoclonius, 4.5" long, VEB Plaho,
1960s-1980s 15-25
Monoclonius, 4.5" long, Marolin, 1990s
(fig. 1-135) 10-15
Pteranodon, 5.5" across, VEB Plaho,
1960s-1980s 15-25
Pteranodon, 5.5" across, Marolin, 1990s
(fig. 1-136) 10-15
Trees, 4 different, VEB Plaho, 1960s-1980s .7-10
Trees, 4 different, Marolin, 1990s (fig. 1-137) 5-8
Tyrannosaurus, 4" tall, VEB Plaho,
1960s-1980s 15-25
Tyrannosaurus, 4" tall, Marolin, 1990s
(fig. 1-138) 10-15

Fig. 1-138: Tyrannosaurus

Fig. 1-137: Tree assortment, by Marolin

Fig. 1-139

MARVEL TRADING CORP.
Vinyl figures 6-8" long, Hong Kong, 1988
(fig. 1-139)

Ankylosaurus	$3-5
Apatosaurus	3-5
Dimetrodon	3-5
Stegosaurus	3-5
Triceratops	3-5
Tyrannosaurus	3-5
Boxed set	20-25

MICROMACHINES
National Geographic series, articulated
plastic miniatures, Galoob, 1998

Set 1: Dinosaur Fossils (3)	$6-10
Set 2: Camptosaurus, Stegosaurus, Compsognatus	6-10
Set 3: Allosaurus, Dilophosaur, Diplodocus	6-10
Set 4: Brachiosaurus, Euoplocephalus, Pachycephalosaurus	6-10
Set 5: T-Rex, Deinonycus, Styracosaurus (fig. 1-140)	10-15
Set 6: Triceratops, Troodon, Spinosaurus	6-10

MILLER
"Waxy Miller Dinosaurs," waxy plastic, 1950s
Note: Large figures measure 3-5" tall.

Brontops, small	$250-450
Brontosaurus, large (fig. 1-141)	195-225
Brontosaurus, small	200-400
Cave diorama background	140-170
Cave people, man, woman and child, 3", each	40-65
Coelodonta (Rhino), large	120-150
Dimetrodon, large (fig. 1-142)	200-250
Dimetrodon, small	200-400

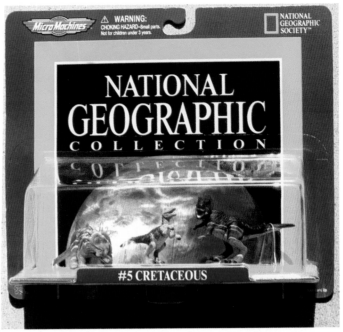

Fig. 1-140: Set 5: T-Rex, Deinonycus, Styracosaurus

Fig. 1-141: Brontosaurus

Fig. 1-142: Dimetrodon

Fig. 1-143: Mastodon

Fig. 1-145: Stegosaurus

Fig. 1-144: Protoceratops

Fig. 1-146: Tyrannosaurus

Mastodon, large (fig. 1-143) $120-150
Megatherium (Sloth), large 200-250
Megatherium, small 200-400
Protoceratops, small (fig. 1-144) 200-400
Pterodactyl (rare) 400-600
Smilodon (Saber-Toothed Tiger) 300-450
Stegosaurus (fig. 1-145) 100-150
Stegosaurus, small 200-400
Trachodon, small 200-400
Triceratops 100-150
Tyrannosaurus (fig. 1-146) 100-150
Tyrannosaurus, small 200-400

Fig. 1-147: Ankylosaurus

Fig. 1-148: Brontosaurus

Fig. 1-149: Diatryma

Fig. 1-150: Kronosaurus

Fig. 1-151: Megatherium

Fig. 1-152: Parasaurolophus

Fig. 1-153: Plateosaurus

Fig. 1-154: Smilodon

MPC
Plastic miniatures, 1964-1970s

Allosaurus $3-4
Ankylosaurus (fig. 1-147) 3-4
Brontosaurus (fig. 1-148) 3-4
Ceratogaulus (horned marmot) 5-10
Cynognathus (sprawled lizard) 5-10
Diatryma, gray plastic (fig. 1-149) 5-10
Dimetrodon 3-4
Dire Wolf 5-10
Glyptodont 5-10
Kronosaurus (fig. 1-150) 5-10
Macraeuchenia (with hanging nose) 5-10
Megatherium (fig. 1-151) 5-10
Moschops 5-10
Parasaurolophus (fig. 1-152) 5-10
Plateosaurus (fig. 1-153) 5-10
Pteranodon 3-4
Smilodon (Saber-Toothed Tiger), gray plastic
    (fig. 1-154) 5-10
Stegosaurus 3-4
Struthiomimus 5-10
Styracosaurus 5-10

Fig. 1-155: Trachodon

Fig. 1-156: Woolly Mammoth

Fig. 1-157: Carded set of "Realistically Detailed Monsters"

Fig. 1-158: Canadian carded sets

Fig. 1-159: Monsters and Mammals with Cavemen playset

Trachodon (fig. 1-155) $5-10
Triceratops 3-4
Tyrannosaurus 3-4
Woolly Mammoth (fig. 1-156) 3-4
Carded set, 12 different MPC "Realistically
    Detailed Monsters," 1964 (fig. 1-157) . . 60-80
Canadian carded sets, each (fig. 1-158) . . 30-45
Playset, Monsters and Mammals with
    Cavemen, boxed, 1960s (fig. 1-159) . . 100-200

Fig. 1-160: Crested Dinosaur

Fig. 1-161: Fin-Back Dinosaur

Fig. 1-162: Flying Reptile

Fig. 1-163: Three-Horned Dinosaur

Fig. 1-164: Thunder Lizard

Fig. 1-165: Tyrant King

Fig. 1-166: Dinosaur Guide

NABISCO CEREAL PREMIUMS
late 1950s

Dinosaurs, 10 different, one inside each box of Wheat Honeys or Rice Honeys, 1-2"

Armored Dinosaur	$7-15
Crested Dinosaur (fig. 1-160)	7-15
Duck-Billed Dinosaur	7-15
Fin-Back Dinosaur (fig. 1-161)	7-15
Flying Reptile (fig. 1-162)	7-15
Reptilian Tank	7-15
Sea Serpent	7-15
Three-Horned Dinosaur (fig. 1-163)	7-15
Thunder Lizard (fig. 1-164)	7-15
Tyrant King (fig. 1-165)	7-15
Full set of 10 figures	100-150
Dinosaur Guide, mail-order cardboard guide (fig. 1-166)	50-75

Pre-Historic Beasts, 8 different, one inside each box of Wheat Honeys or Rice Honeys, silver plastic, 1-2"

American Mastodon (Woolly Elephant) (fig. 1-167)	$7-15
Baluchitherium	7-15
Barylambda	7-15
Giant Pig (fig. 1-168)	7-15
Giant Rhino	7-15
Giraffe Camel (fig. 1-169)	7-15
Macreuchenia	7-15
Smilodon (Saber-Toothed Tiger) (fig. 1-170)	7-15
Full set of 8 figures	60-75

Fig. 1-167: American Mastodon

Fig. 1-168: Giant Pig

Fig. 1-169: Giraffe Camel

Fig. 1-170: Smilodon

ONE MILLION B.C.
Mego, 1976

Dimetrodon $100-250
Grok, 8" 25-45
Hairy Rhino 100-250
Mada, 8" 25-45
Om, 8" 25-45
Trag, 8" 25-45
Tyrannosaur (fig. 1-171) 200-450
Zon, 8" 25-45

Fig. 1-171: Tyrannosaur

Figs. 1-172 and 1-173

Fig. 1-174: Brontosaurus

ORSENIGO
Rubber figures, made in Italy, 1960s
(figs. 1-172 and 1-173)

Ankylosaurus, brown and black,
    large size $200-250
Ankylosaurus, grayish brown rubber,
    small size 75-150
Brontosaurus, gray and black rubber,
    large size (fig. 1-174) 200-250
Brontosaurus, brown and black,
    small size 75-150
Caveman and cavewoman, small size only 75-150
Dimetrodon, green and black, legs out
    flat, rubber, large size (fig. 1-175) . . . 200-250
Dimetrodon, green with white teeth, legs
    and head held upright, small size 75-150
Stegosaurus, green rubber, large size
    (fig. 1-176) 200-250
Stegosaurus, small size 75-150
Triceratops, large size 200-250
Triceratops, dark brown with white teeth,
    small size 75-150
Tyrannosaurus, large size 200-250
Tyrannosaurus, brown and black with
    white teeth, yellow eye, small size 75-150

Fig. 1-175: Dimetrodon

Fig. 1-176: Stegosaurus

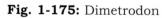

Fig. 1-178 Definitely Dinosaurs! set

Fig. 1-177: Definitely Dinosaurs! set

PLAYSKOOL
Hollow vinyl figures, 1980s-1990s

Definitely Dinosaurs!, jointed figures marked with circular brontosaurus logo. Originally packaged with a caveman or cavewoman and their own special storybook, 1987-1988.
(figs. 1-177 and 1-178)

Anatosaurus, "Ana," #3020, 11" long,
1987 . . . . $5-10
Anatosaurus, #3119, 1992 4-8
Ankylosaurus, "Lozar," #3000, 1987
(fig. 1-179) 5-10
Apatosaurus, "Pat," #3050, 1987
(fig. 1-180) 5-10
Caveman or Cavewoman, several styles, each
(figs. 1-181 to 1-183) 3-5

Fig. 1-179: Ankylosaurus

Fig. 1-180: Apatosaurus

Figs. 1-181, 1-182, 1-183: Caveman and Cavewoman, in various styles

Fig. 1-185: Dimetrodon

Fig. 1-186: Moschops, "Elgar"

Fig. 1-184: Deinonychus, "Dragar"

Fig. 1-187: Protoceratops, "Cera"

Fig. 1-188: Spinosaurus, "Spiney"

Deinonychus, "Dragar," #3003, 1987
 (fig. 1-184) $5-10
Deinonychus, #3122, 1992 4-8
Dimetrodon, "Trodar," #3007, 1987-1988 . . 5-10
Dimetrodon, #3132, 1992 (fig. 1-185) 4-8
Moschops, "Elgar," #3005, 7", 1987-1988
 (fig. 1-186) 5-10
Pachycephalosaurus, "Zalmar," #3014,
 1987-1988 5-10
Parasaurolophus, "Parax," #3026,
 1987-1988 5-10
Polocanthus, "Glutron," #3-13, 1987-1988 . 5-10
Protoceratops, "Cera," #3001, 7" long,
 1987-1988 (fig. 1-187) 5-10
Protoceratops, #3130, 7" long, 1992 4-8
Psittacosaurus, "Takor," #3006, 1987-1988 5-10
Psittacosaurus, #3131, 1992 4-8
Spinosaurus, "Spiney," #3025, 1987-1988
 (fig. 1-188) 5-10
Stegosaurus, "Spike," #3023, 11" long, 1987
 (fig. 1-189) 5-10
Stegosaurus, #3118, 1992 4-8
Struthiomimus, "Strimus," #3002, 1987
 (fig. 1-190) 5-10
Triceratops, "Dozer," #3022, 1987 5-10
Triceratops, #3117, 1992 4-8
Tyrannosaurus, "Tyro," #3055, 1987
 (fig. 1-191) 5-10
Tyrannosaurus, #3113, 1992 4-8
Ultrasaurus, "Ultrar," #3056, orange, 30",
 1989 15-25

Fig. 1-189: Stegosaurus, "Spike"

Fig. 1-190: Struthiomimus, "Strimus"

Fig. 1-191: Tyrannosaurus, "Tyro"

Fig. 1-192: Ankylosaurus

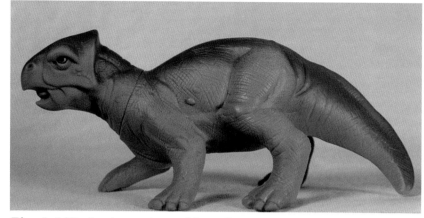

Fig. 1-193: Leptoceratops, "Jexar"

Miniatures

Ankylosaurus, "Thondor," rust-colored
  with orange, miniature, 1988 . . . . $4-8
Ankylosaurus, light and dark green,
  5.5" long, Wendy's 2nd series promo
  piece, 1988 (fig. 1-192) 3-6
Ankylosaurus, yellow and brown,
  miniature, 1991 2-4
Anatosaurus, yellow with orange paint,
  5.5" long, Wendy's promo piece, 1988 4-8
Anatosaurus, gray and brown, miniature,
  1991 2-4
Apatosaurus, light blue with darker blue
  paint, 6" long, Wendy's promo piece,
  1988 3-6
Apatosaurus, pink with purple paint,
  6" long, Wendy's 2nd series promo
  piece, 1988 3-6
Apatosaurus, cream-colored with brown
  paint, miniature, 1991 2-4
Brachiosaurus, "Trimor," yellow and green,
  miniature, 1988 5-10
Brachiosaurus, lime green with green paint,
  miniature, 1991 2-4
Ceratosaurus, "Zune," tan with mustard
  yellow paint, miniature, 1988 4-8
Ceratosaurus, light and dark green, Wendy's
  2nd series promo piece, 1988 4-8
Ceratosaurus, green and yellow, miniature,
  1991 2-4
Leptoceratops, "Jexar," light and dark blue,
  miniature, 1988 (fig. 1-193) 4-8
Leptoceratops, off-white with blue paint,
  miniature, 1991 2-4
Parasaurolophus, "Flexar," pink and purple,
  miniature, 1988 4-8
Parasaurolophus, blue, 4.5", Wendy's 2nd
  series promo piece, 1988 (fig. 1-194) . . . $3-6

Fig. 1-194: Parasaurolophus

Parasaurolophus, light blue with darker
  blue paint, miniature, 1991 2-4
Stegosaurus, green with yellow back, 3",
  Wendy's 2nd series promo piece,
  1988 (fig. 1-195) 3-6
Stegosaurus, "Massor," light and dark
  green, miniature, 1988 4-8
Stegosaurus, lavender and purple,
  miniature, 1991 2-4
Triceratops, light green with darker green
  paint, 5.5" long, Wendy's promo piece,
  1988 3-6
Triceratops, brown w/orange paint, 5.5" long,
  Wendy's 2nd series promo piece, 1988
  (fig. 1-196) 3-6
Triceratops, light and dark brown,
  miniature, 1991 2-4
Tyrannosaurus, lavender w/blue paint,
  5.5" long, Wendy's promo piece, 1988
  (fig. 1-197) 5-10

Fig. 1-195: Stegosaurus

Fig. 1-198: Hadrosaurus

Fig. 1-196: Triceratops

Fig. 1-199: Kronosaurus

PREHISTORIC MONSTERS
Boxed plastic miniatures, ELM Toys, 1962

Hadrosaurus, box is 1.5" x 2.5" (fig. 1-198) $8-12
Kronosaurus, box is 1.5" x 2.5" (fig. 1-199) . 8-12
Trachodon, box is 1.5" x 2.5" 8-12

Fig. 1-197: Tyrannosaurus

Fig. 1-200: Chasmosaurus

Fig. 1-201: Lambeosaurus

Fig. 1-202: Stegosaurus

Fig. 1-203: Stenopterygis

ROYAL ONTARIO MUSEUM (ROM)
Gray plastic, set of 8, 1977

Albertosaurus, 3" $5-10
Chasmosaurus, 4" long (fig. 1-200) 5-10
Diplodocus, 8.5" long 5-10
Lambeosaurus, 6" long (fig. 1-201) 5-10
Parasaurolophus, 6" long 5-10
Pteranodon 7-15
Stegosaurus, 4" long (fig. 1-202) 5-10
Stenopterygis (fish), 3.5" long (fig. 1-203) . . 7-15

Multicolored re-issues

Albertosaurus, 3" $3-5
Chasmosaurus, 4" long 3-5
Diplodocus, 8.5" long 3-5
Lambeosaurus, 6" long 3-5
Pteranodon 3-5
Stegosaurus, 4" long 3-5
Full set of 6 figures 25-35

Fig. 1-205: Giant Anteater

Fig. 1-206: Mammoth

"RU"
In circle logo, plastic miniatures, 1-2", made in China, 1996

Cave Bear (fig. 1-204) $2-4
Giant Anteater (fig. 1-205) 2-4
Mammoth (fig. 1-206) 2-4
Marsupial Cat 2-4
Oreodont 2-4

Fig. 1-204: Cave Bear

Fig. 1-207: Ceratosaurus

Fig. 1-208: Mamenchisaurus

Fig. 1-209: Therizinosaurus

Fig. 1-210: Yangchuanosaurus

SAFARI LTD.
Painted vinyl figures, Miami, Florida, 1990s
Wild Safari

Allosaurus, 5.75" $5-6
Apatosaurus, 9" 6-10
Brachiosaurus, 9" 6-10
Carcharodontsaurus, 7.5" 5-6
Ceratosaurus, 5.5" (fig. 1-207) 4-6
Pachycephalosaurus, 5.5" 4-6
Parasaurolophus, 6.5" 4-6
Stegosaurus, 5.75" 4-6
Styracosaurus, 6.25" 4-6
Triceratops, 7" 5-6
Tyrannosaurus Rex, 7" 5-6
Utahraptor, 5-6" 5-6
Set of 6 Wild Safari baby dinosaurs 10-15

Missing Links

Neanderthal Family (3 figures) $12-15
Saber-Toothed Tiger 5-8
Woolly Mammoth 10-15
Woolly Mammoth baby 3-5
Woolly Rhino 10-15

Ely Kish Dinosaurs of China

Mamenchisaurus, 27" long (fig. 1-208) . . .$25-35
Therizinosaurus, 1/40 scale, 7"
    (fig. 1-209) 8-12
Yangchuanosaurus, 1/40 scale, 7.5"
    (fig. 1-210) 8-12

Fig. 1-211: Ankylosaurus with long tail

Fig. 1-213: Diatryma (Urvogel)

Fig. 1-214: Elasmosaurus

Fig. 1-212: Brontosaurus (Ursaurier)

Fig. 1-215: Stegosaurus (Stegsaurier)

SCHLEICH
Vinyl and rubbery figures, Germany, 1980s-1990s
*Standard Line, unpainted solid colors,
average 3" long, 1980s, discontinued*

Ankylosaurus with long tail (Stachelsaurier) $2-4
Brontosaurus (Ursaurier) 2-4
Diatryma (Urvogel) 2-4
Elasmosaurus (Schwimmsaurier) 2-4
Stegosaurus (Stegsaurier) 2-4
Triceratops (Kragensaurier) 2-4
Tyrannosaurus (Konigsaurier) 2-4
Turtle with long neck (Panzersaurier) 2-4
(Kammsaurier) 2-4

*Standard Line, painted vinyl, average
3" long, 1990s, still available*

Ankylosaurus with long tail (Stachelsaurier)
(fig. 1-211) $1-2
Brontosaurus (Ursaurier) (fig. 1-212) 1-2
Diatryma (Urvogel) (fig. 1-213) 1-2
Elasmosaurus (Schwimmsaurier) (fig. 1-214) .1-2
Stegosaurus (Stegsaurier) (fig. 1-215) 1-2
Triceratops (Kragensaurier) (fig. 1-216) 1-2
Tyrannosaurus (Konigsaurier) (fig. 1-217) . . . 1-2
Turtle with long neck (Panzersaurier)
(fig. 1-218) 1-2
(Kammsaurier) (fig. 1-219) 1-2

Fig. 1-216: Triceratops (Kragensaurier)

Fig. 1-217: Tyranno-saurus (Konigsaurier)

Fig. 1-218: Turtle with long neck (Panzersaurier)

Fig. 1-219: (Kammsaurier)

Fig. 1-220: Ankylosaurus

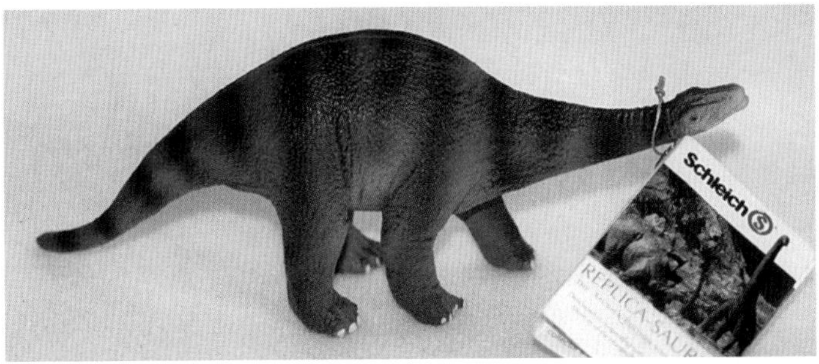

Fig. 1-225: Apatosaurus baby

Fig. 1-221: Diatryma

Fig. 1-222: Dimetrodon

Fig. 1-223: Triceratops

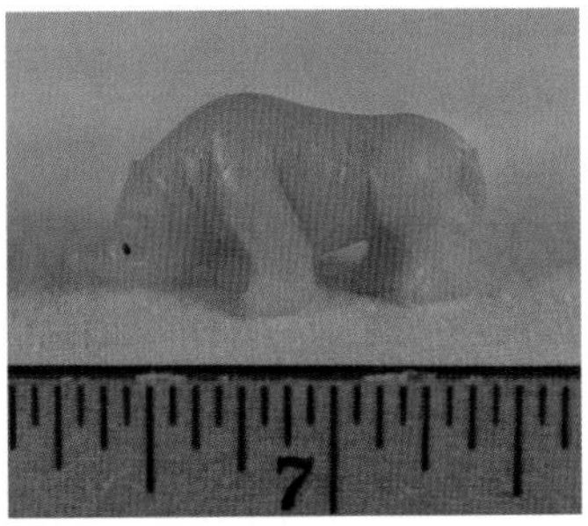

Fig. 1-224: Woolly Rhino

Fig. 1-226: Brachiosaurus

*Miniature rubbery figures with painted
highlights, 1", 1990s, still available*

Ankylosaurus (fig. 1-220) . . . . 25-50¢
Diatryma (fig. 1-221) . . . . 25-50¢
Dimetrodon (fig. 1-222) . . . . 25-50¢
Elasmosaurus . . . . 25-50¢
Mammoth . . . . 25-50¢
Plateosaurus . . . . 25-50¢
Prehistoric Snake . . . . 25-50¢
Triceratops (fig. 1-223) . . . . 25-50¢
Tyrannosaurus Rex . . . . 25-50¢
Woolly Rhino (fig. 1-224) . . . . 25-50¢

*Replica-Saurus series, painted vinyl,
1/40 scale with string tag, 1996*

Apatosaurus baby, 7.5" (fig. 1-225) $25-50
Brachiosaurus, 13" long (fig. 1-226) 30-40
Ceratosaurus, 7.5" (fig. 1-227) 25-35
Parasaurolophus, 4" (fig. 1-228) 25-35

Fig. 1-227: Ceratosaurus

Fig. 1-228: Parasaurolophus

Fig. 1-229: Spinosaurus

Fig. 1-230: Stegosaurus

Fig. 1-231: Triceratops

Spinosaurus, 9.5" long (fig. 1-229) $25-35
Stegosaurus, 8" long (fig. 1-230) 25-35
Triceratops, 9" (fig. 1-231) 25-35
Tyrannosaurus, 9" (fig. 1-232) 25-35
Full set of 8 figures 160-220

SHREDDIES
Cereal premiums, England, 20 pieces, tan plastic with long oval base, late 1950s (fig. 1-233)

Note: Other foreign versions were also released in different colors.

Apatosaurus $20-40
Crocodile 20-40
Dimetrodon 20-40
Diplodocus (Elasmosaurus) 20-40
Ichthyosaurus (fig. 1-234) 20-40
Iguanodon 20-40
Mosasaurus 20-40
Nothosaurus .20-40
Paleotherium 20-40
Plateosaurus 20-40
Plesiosaurus 20-40
Prehistoric bird on branch 20-40
Pteranodon .20-40
Protoceratops 20-40
Sphenacodon 20-40
Stegosaurus 20-40
Triceratops (fig. 1-235) 20-40
Tylosaurus .20-40
Tyrannosaurus 20-40
Woolly Mammoth 20-40
Woolly Rhino (fig. 1-236) 20-40

Fig. 1-232: Tyrannosaurus

Fig. 1-233: Shreddies premiums

Fig. 1-234: Ichthyosaurus

Fig. 1-235: Triceratops

Fig. 1-236: Woolly Rhino

Fig. 1-237: SRG figures

SRG
Plastic versions of 1940s metal figures, 1960s (fig. 1-237)

Brontosaurus, gray plastic,
    smooth body $20-40
Dimetrodon, gray plastic 20-40
Mammoth, gray plastic 20-40
Stegosaurus, gray plastic (not shown) 20-40
Triceratops, gray plastic 20-40
Tyrannosaurus, big outstretched hands,
    gray plastic 20-40

STARLUX
French, painted hard plastic figures, early 1970s-present

(note: some listed with French names)

Acantopholis $5-10
Allosaurus, discontinued 8-15
Alticamelus, discontinued 8-15
Anatosaurus (fig. 1-238) 5-10
Andrewsaurchus 5-10
Archelon 5-10
Arsinoitherium (fig. 1-239) 5-10
Aurochs 5-10
Baluchitherium, discontinued 8-15
Bradysaurus, discontinued 15-25
Brontotherium, discontinued (fig. 1-240) . . 8-15
Brontosaurus 5-10
Cave Bear 5-10
Caveman carrying animal 5-10
Caveman (Cro-Magnon) with necklace, club .5-10
Caveman (mammoth hunter) holding
    rock overhead 5-10
Caveman (mammoth hunter) standing
    with spear down 5-10
Caveman squatting with rock 5-10
Caveman swinging club 5-10
Caveman kneeling with club 5-10
Caveman (Neanderthal) lifting spear 5-10
Caveman (mammoth hunter) with arm
    and spear raised $5-10
Caveman (Neanderthal) with club raised
    over head 5-10
Caveman with both hands on spear 5-10
Cavewoman (Neanderthal), sitting with baby   5-10
Cavewoman walking with baby 5-10
Cephalaspis (fig. 1-241) 5-10
Coelophysis, discontinued 8-15
Corythosaurus 5-10
Cynognathus 5-10
Deinonychus 5-10
Diatryma, discontinued 8-15
Dicraeosaurus 5-10
Dimetrodon 5-10
Deinotherium (fig. 1-242) 5-10
Diplocaulus pair, discontinued 8-15
Diplodocus, original version, discontinued 20-30
Diplodocus, current version (fig. 1-243) . . . 5-10
Drepanaspis (fig. 1-244) 5-10
Edaphosaurus (fig. 1-245) 5-10
Endothiodon, discontinued 8-15
Eohippus (fig. 1-246) 5-10
Euparkeria 5-10
Euplocephalus (fig. 1-247) 5-10
Eusthenopteron (fig. 1-248) 5-10
Giant Elk 5-10
Gigantocamelus, discontinued 8-15

Fig. 1-238: Anatosaurus

Fig. 1-240: Brontotherium

Fig. 1-242: Deinotherium

Fig. 1-239: Arsinoitherium

Fig. 1-241: Cephalaspis

Fig. 1-243: Diplodocus

Fig. 1-244: Drepanaspis

Fig. 1-246: Eohippus

Fig. 1-245: Edaphosaurus

Fig. 1-247: Euplocephalus

Fig. 1-248: Eusthenopteron

Fig. 1-249: Labyrinthodont

Fig. 1-250: Machairodus

Glyptodon, discontinued $8-15
Ichthyosaurus 5-10
Ichthyostega, discontinued 8-15
Iguanodon 5-10
Labyrinthodont, discontinued (fig. 1-249) . . 8-15
Machairodus (fig. 1-250) 5-10
Mammoth, original version, discontinued . 20-30
Mammoth, current version (fig. 1-251) 5-10
Mastodonsaurus, discontinued (fig. 1-252) . 8-15

Fig. 1-251: Mammoth

Fig. 1-252: Mastodonsaurus

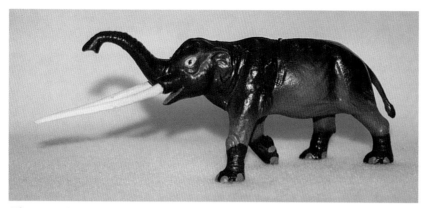

Fig. 1-253: Mastodonte

Fig. 1-255: Megatherium

Fig. 1-254: Megalosaurus

Fig. 1-256: Moropus

Fig. 1-257: Ouranosaurus

Fig. 1-258:
Pachycephalosaurus

Fig. 1-259: Parasaurolophus

Fig. 1-260: Platybelodon

Fig. 1-261: Rhamphorhynchus

Fig. 1-262: Rhinoceros

Fig. 1-265:
Tyrannosaurus

Fig. 1-266:
Uintatherium

Fig. 1-263: Shantungosaurus

Fig. 1-264: Spinosaurus (crawling)

Pteranodon $5-10
Pterodactyl (hanging from branch) 5-10
Rhamphorhynchus (fig. 1-261) 5-10
Rhinoceros (fig. 1-262) 5-10
Saltoposuchus 5-10
Scelidosaurus 5-10
Scolosaurus 5-10
Scutosaurus, discontinued 8-15
Shantungosaurus (fig. 1-263) 5-10
Spinosaurus (crawling) (fig. 1-264) 5-10
Spirifer, discontinued 8-15
Stegosaurus 5-10
Struthiomimus, discontinued 20-25
Styracosaurus 5-10
Synthetoceras, discontinued 8-15
Tanystropheus 5-10
Tanystropheius chassant 5-10
Triceratops 5-10
Trilobite, discontinued 12-20
Tylosaurus 5-10
Tyrannosaurus (fig. 1-265) 5-10
Uintatherium (fig. 1-266) 5-10

Fig. 1-267: Brontosaurus

Fig. 1-269: Moschops

Fig. 1-268: Iguanodon

Fig. 1-270: Parasaurolophus

SUPERIOR
Marbled plastic figures (brown, tan or green) from Marx molds, low distribution, now discontinued, 1980s

Allosaurus, 60 mm $5-8
Ankylosaurus, 60 mm 5-8
Brontosaurus, 60 mm (fig. 1-267) 8-12
Caveman holding rock over head, 45 mm . . . 2-4
Caveman walking with club, 45 mm 2-4
Caveman with club, knife, 45 mm 2-4
Caveman with rock, flint, 45 mm 2-4
Caveman skinning rabbit, 45 mm 2-4
Caveman squatting with spear, 45 mm . . . 2-4
Cynognaurus, 60 mm 5-8
Hadrosaurus, 60 mm 5-8
Iguanodon, 60 mm (fig. 1-268) 5-8
Kronosaurus, 60 mm 5-8
Megatherium, 60 mm 8-12
Moschops, 60 mm (fig. 1-269) 5-8
Parasaurolophus, 60 mm (fig. 1-270) 5-8
Pteranodon, 60 mm (fig. 1-271) 5-8

Fig. 1-271: Pteranodon

Fig. 1-272: Smilodon

Fig. 1-273: Rulers of the Earth, 60-piece boxed set

Smilodon (Saber-Toothed Tiger), 60 mm
(fig. 1-272) $8-12
Stegosaurus, 60 mm 5-8
Struthiomimus, 60 mm 5-8
Styracosaurus, 60 mm 5-8
Trachodon, 60 mm 5-8
Tyrannosaurus, pot-belly, 60 mm 8-12
Woolly Mammoth, 60 mm 8-12
Boxed set, Rulers of the Earth, 60 pieces with
Mountain (fig. 1-273) 175-225

SYNTHETIC FLESH DINOSAURS
Rubbery models by Jary Lesser, 1993

Allosaurus (from *One Million Years BC*) . .$35-50
Stegosaurus (from *King Kong*) 35-50
Styracosaurus (from *Son of Kong*) 35-50

TEENAGE MUTANT NINJA DINO TURTLES
Action figures, Playmates, 1997

Ankyl Leo $3-6
Pterano Don 3-6
Stego Ralph 3-6
Tricera Mike 3-6
Tyranno Shredder 3-6

THEN AND NOW
Plastic figures with skeletons, carded, Galoob, 1993

Brontosaurus $12-18
Euoplocephalus (fig. 1-274) 12-18
Ouranosaurus (Spinosaurus) (figs. 1-275
and 1-276) 12-18
Parasaurolophus 12-18

Fig. 1-274: Euoplocephalus

Figs. 1-275 and 1-276: Ouranosaurus

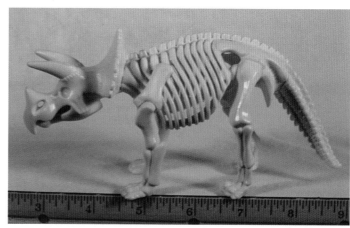

Figs. 1-277 and 1-278: Triceratops

Figs. 1-279 and 1-280: Stegosaurus

Fig. 1-281: Dilophosaurus

Triceratops (figs. 1-277 and 1-278) $12-18
Stegosaurus (figs. 1-279 and 1-280) 12-18
Tyrannosaurus 12-18

THUNDER BEASTS
Boxed action figures, Sky Kids, 1993

Apatosaurus, medium $8-12
Callovasaurus, medium 8-12
Corythosaurus, small 5-8
Dimetrodon, small 5-8
Dilophosaurus, medium (fig. 1-281) 8-12
Euoplocephalus, medium 8-12
Ornithosuchus, small 5-8
Pachycephalosaurus, large (fig. 1-282) . . . 10-15
Parasaurolophus, small (fig. 1-283) 5-8
Protoceratops, small (fig. 1-284) 5-8
Saurolophus, small 5-8
Stegosaurus, large (fig. 1-285) 10-15
Styracosaurus, small 5-8
Triceratops, small (fig. 1-286) 5-8
Tyrannosaurus, large (fig. 1-287) 10-15
Velociraptor, large 10-15
Velociraptor, small 5-8

Fig. 1-282:
Pachycephalosaurus

Fig. 1-283:
Parasaurolophus

Fig. 1-284: Protoceratops

Fig. 1-285: Stegosaurus

Fig. 1-286: Triceratops

Fig. 1-287: Tyrannosaurus

Fig. 1-288: Timmee Toys miniatures

Fig. 1-289: Mammoth

TIMMEE TOYS
Colored plastic miniatures, 1960s-present
(fig. 1-288)

Ankylosaurus, small scale, 1960s $1-2
Ankylosaurus, smoother, more detailed,
   1970s 1-2
Brontosaurus, gray or blue, head up, 2",
   original mold 2-3
Brontosaurus, golden brown, head down,
   2", original mold 2-3
Brontosaurus, smoother, more detailed,
   1970s 1-2
Brontosaurus, smaller scale, tail curled
   up, head looks backward, 1960s 1-2
Caveman (3 different designs), original
   mold, 2", each 2-3
Dimetrodon, golden brown, 2", original mold   2-3
Dimetrodon, small scale, 1960s 1-2
Dimetrodon, smoother, more detailed, 1970s   1-2
Mammoth, added to the line in 1970s
   (fig. 1-289) 1-2
Plateosaurus, small scale, 1960s 1-2
Pterodactyl (Pteranodon), small scale, 1960s   1-2
Seymouria, small scale, 1960s 1-2
Smilodon, added to the line in 1970s 1-2
Stegosaurus, small scale, 1960s 1-2
Stegosaurus, smoother, more detailed, 1970s   1-2
Trachodon (duckbill), blue, 2", original mold . 2-3
Trachodon, smoother, more detailed, 1970s .   1-2
Triceratops, 2", original mold 2-3

Triceratops, small scale, 1960s $1-2
Triceratops, smoother, more detailed, 1970s . 1-2
Tyrannosaurus (looks like Allosaurus), 2",
    original mold 2-3
Tyrannosaurus, small scale, 1960s 1-2
Tyrannosaurus, smoother, more detailed,
    1970s 1-2
Bagged set, Animals from Prehistoric Days,
    with large Timmee logo on header 40-50
Bagged set, no. 486, cartoon dinosaur
    on header card, 1960s 40-50
Bagged set, Dinosaurs with Volcano, 1990s . 2-3
Boxed set, Dinosaur Mountain, 66 pieces,
    1993 (fig. 1-290) 12-18

TIMPO MODEL TOYS
England, 1950s-1960s
(fig. 1-291)

Boxed set, 6 hand-painted plastic figures
    (fig. 1-292) $275-325
Brontosaurus, green plastic 30-40
Dimetrodon, dark plastic 30-40
Giant Sloth, dark plastic 30-40
Stegosaurus, dark plastic 30-40
Triceratops, yellow plastic 30-40
Tyrannosaurus, yellow plastic
    (fig. 1-293) 30-40

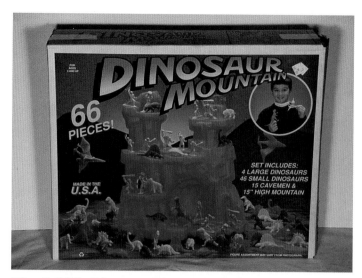

Fig. 1-290: Dinosaur Mountain boxed set

Fig. 1-291: Timpo Model Toys

TOPPS
Green-, gray-, and brown-colored
plastic, 2", 1980s
(fig. 1-294)

Allosaurus $2-5
Ankylosaurus (fig. 1-295) 2-5
Brontosaurus (fig. 1-296) 2-5
Dimetrodon 2-5
Hadrosaur (duckbill) 2-5
Iguanodon 2-5
Parasaurolophus 2-5
Plesiosaur 2-5
Pteranodon 2-5
Stegosaurus (fig. 1-297) 2-5
Triceratops 2-5
Tyrannosaurus 2-5
Unopened Box (fig. 1-298) 20-30
Unopened Pack (fig. 1-299) 4-8

Fig. 1-292: Boxed set of 6 hand-painted plastic figures

Fig. 1-293: Tyrannosaurus

Fig. 1-294: Topps Set

Fig. 1-298: Unopened Box

Fig. 1-295: Ankylosaurus

Fig. 1-299: Unopened Pack

Fig. 1-296: Brontosaurus

Fig. 1-297: Stegosaurus

Fig. 1-300: Allosaurus

Fig. 1-301: Brontosaurus

Fig. 1-302: Pachycephalosaurus

Fig. 1-303: Parasaurolophus

Fig. 1-304: Plesiosaurus

Fig. 1-305: Spinosaurus

TSUKUDA DINOSAUR SERIES
1/30 scale, painted vinyl, bead eyes, Tsukuda Hobby, 1980s

Allosaurus, DS-12 (fig. 1-300) $50-75
Anatosaurus (duckbill), DS-08 50-75
Ankylosaurus, DS-06 50-75
Brontosaurus, DS-01, 20" long
  (fig. 1-301) 95-125
Pachycephalosaurus, DS-10 (fig. 1-302) . . 50-75
Parasaurolophus, DS-09 (fig. 1-303) 60-80
Plesiosaurus, DS-11 (fig. 1-304) 50-75
Spinosaurus, DS-07, 7.5" (fig. 1-305) 60-80
Stegosaurus, DS-04 (fig. 1-306) 50-75
Styracosaurus, DS-05 60-80
Triceratops, DS-02 (fig. 1-307) 50-75
Tyrannosaurus, DS-03 (fig. 1-308) 50-75

Fig. 1-306: Stegosaurus

Fig. 1-308: Tyrannosaurus

Fig. 1-307: Triceratops

Fig. 1-309: Ankylosaurus

Fig. 1-311: Apatosaurus

U.K.R.D.
Soft vinyl figures, bright colors, China, early 1990s

Ankylosaurus, orange with open mouth,
5.5" long, 1992 (fig. 1-309) $3-5
Apatosaurus, green striped, 6" tall, 1991
(fig. 1-310) 5-8
Apatosaurus, blue, 6" long, 1992
(fig. 1-311) 3-5

Fig. 1-310: Apatosaurus

Fig. 1-312: Dimetrodon

Fig. 1-313: Dimetrodon

Fig. 1-317: Tyrannosaurus

Fig. 1-314: Iguanodon

Fig. 1-318: Tyrannosaurus

Fig. 1-315: Protoceratops

Dimetrodon, orange and yellow with
   white teeth, 5.5", 1992 (fig. 1-312) $3-5
Dimetrodon, mauve, 4", 1993 (fig. 1-313) . . . 2-4
Iguanodon, yellow-green, 3.5", 1992
   (fig. 1-314) 3-5
Protoceratops, orange and blue, 6.5", 1991
   (fig. 1-315) 5-8
Triceratops, yellow-green, 5.5", 1992
   (fig. 1-316) 3-5
Tyrannosaurus, blue, 4", 1992 (fig. 1-317) . . 3-5
Tyrannosaurus, brown and black, 6.5",
   1991 (fig. 1-318) 5-8

VEB PLAHO
(See Marolin/VEB Plaho)

Fig. 1-316: Triceratops

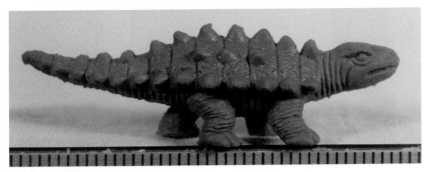

Fig. 1-319: Ankylosaurus

Fig. 1-322: Tyrannosaurus

Fig. 1-320: Pteranodon

Fig. 1-321: Stegosaurus

WHEETO'S, BRITISH CEREAL PREMIUMS
12 figural erasers, 1990s

Ankylosaurus, 2.5" long (fig. 1-319) $2-5
Brachiosaurus, 5" long 2-5
Dimetrodon, 2.5" long 2-5
Ichthyosaurus, 2.5" long 2-5
Lambeosaurus, 2.25" long 2-5
Mammoth, 2" long 2-5
Plesiosaur, 2" long 2-5
Pteranodon, 2.5" long (fig. 1-320) 2-5
Stegosaurus, 2.5" long (fig. 1-321) 2-5
Triceratops, 2.5" long 2-5
Tylosaurus, 2.5" long 2-5
Tyrannosaurus, 2.5" long (fig. 1-322) 2-5

Fig. 1-323: Kronosaurus

WINNECO INDUSTRIES
MPC re-issues, slightly smaller and with curled tails, late 1960s

Allosaurus $2-3
Ankylosaurus 2-3
Brontosaurus 2-3
Cynognathus 2-3
Dimetrodon 2-3
Iguanodon 2-3
Kronosaurus (fig. 1-323) 2-3
Plateosaurus 2-3
Pteranodon 2-3
Styracosaurus 2-3
Trachodon (fig. 1-324) 2-3

Fig. 1-324: Trachodon

Fig. 1-325: Bag of Fun, header card for bagged plastic dinosaurs

Fig. 1-326: Brontosaurus

Fig. 1-327: Creatures of the World: Dinosaur Collection

Fig. 1-328: Brontosaurus, purple plastic, hollow dimestore toy

Fig. 1-329: Mammoth, brown vinyl w/melon eye

Triceratops $2-3
Tyrannosaurus 2-3
Bag of Fun, header card for bagged plastic
     dinosaurs, Winneco, 1960s, full bag
     (fig. 1-325) 25-35

MISCELLANEOUS VINYL AND PLASTIC FIGURES

Brontosaurus, yellow plastic, School Toy
     Brand, 1960s, rare (fig. 1-326) $30-50
Creatures of the World: Dinosaur
     Collection, boxed set of 5, Imperial,
     1980s-90s (fig. 1-327) 4-8
Figure, Brontosaurus, purple plastic, 3.5",
     Marx re-issue, 1970s 2-3
Figure, Brontosaurus, purple plastic,
     hollow dimestore toy (fig. 1-328) . . 50¢-$1.00
Figure, Mammoth, brown vinyl w/melon
     eye, line around middle, 9" long, Imperial,
     1989 (fig. 1-329) 8-12
Figure, Saber-Toothed Tiger, Zabu, 6",
     Savage Land Series, Marvel, Toy Biz,
     1997 4-7
Figure, Stegosaurus, vinyl, red with green
     stripes, open mouth, 7.5", "CE, China"
     (fig. 1-330) 3-5

Fig. 1-330: Stegosaurus, vinyl, red with green stripes, open mouth

Fig. 1-331: Triceratops, large brown plastic figure, open mouth

Fig. 1-333: Gum machine toys, snap-together Monster Dinosaur skeletons

Fig. 1-332: Gum machine toys, colored mammals, variety

Fig. 1-334: Set of 10 dinosaurs, various colors

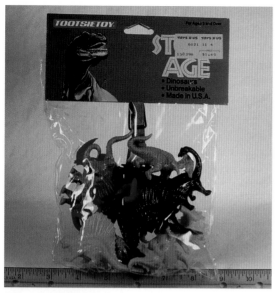

Fig. 1-335: Stone Age, bagged dinosaur set (re-issues)

Fig. 1-336: Centrosaurus

Fig. 1-337: Eudoplocephalus

Stone Age, bagged dinosaur set, re-issues
of 1950s Ajax figures, Tootsietoy, 1993
(fig. 1-335) $1-3

*Unknown manufacturer, soft vinyl dinosaur series,
made in Mexico, 1990s*

Centrosaurus, green spotted, 5.5" long
(fig. 1-336) $5-10
Eudoplocephalus, beige and rust-colored
armored dinosaur, 5" long (fig. 1-337) . . . 5-10
Parasaurolophus, green splotched, 5.5"
long (fig. 1-338) 5-10
Tyrannosaurus, brown, on base with tail
up, 6.5" long (fig. 1-339) 5-10
Utahraptor, striped, on base, 5.5" long
(fig. 1-340) 5-10

Fig. 1-338: Parasaurolophus

Fig. 1-339: Tyrannosaurus

Fig. 1-340: Utahraptor

MARX
PLASTIC FIGURES AND PREHISTORIC PLAYSETS

BY JOE DEMARCO

Fig. M-1: Marx 1950s-era playset

Special thanks to Glenn Ridenour of the Fun House Toy Company—the Marx plastics expert—for his input and inspiration in the compilation of this section . . . and the collective input of Mike Fredericks, Riff Smith, Bruce Darling, Larry Blincoe, and Jack Arata.

The history of Marx dinosaurs is a fascinating subject. For many dinosaur enthusiasts and collectors, the Marx dinosaur models were the beginning of it all—the genesis of a lifetime of interest and passionate obsession for the intrigue of prehistoric life.

It is believed that all "original" Marx dinosaur figures date from approximately 1955 to 1963. In order to fully understand or engage in any informative dialogue concerning the Marx models, one must first understand how they were produced. Unlike today's lavish scale model reproductions, the Marx dinosaurs were released by mold groupings—not as single pieces. It is important to understand what pieces belong to each of these groups, and the relationship of one group to another, before we launch into an indepth description and history. Each Marx mold was given a number, which is noted below in parentheses. To my knowledge, the known Marx molds can be delineated as follows:

1. Large mold group (PL749), circa 1955—
Brontosaurus, Pot-Belly T-Rex, Kronosaurus

2. Medium mold group (PL750), circa 1955—
Allosaurus, Hadrosaurus, Trachodon, Ankylosaurus, Stegosaurus, Pteranodon

3. Small mold group (PL755), circa 1955
Triceratops, Cynognathus, Plateosaurus, Sphenacodon, Dimetrodon.

This mold contained two images of the Dimetrodon and two of the Plateosaur. So, in effect, this was a mold with seven dinosaurs. Amazingly, there is a very slight mold variation on these two extra pieces. So, the Dimetrodon and Plateosaurus, themselves, have slight variances:

Dimetrodon: On the tail inscription, one has a tail line pointing between the "n" and "g" of the word "long." The other has the tail line pointing directly at the "n."

Plateosaurus: In the "20' long" inscription on the dinosaur's tail, one version has the "2" and "0" being level, while in the other, the "2" is noticeably higher. These are minor variances, but variances nonetheless.

4. Revised mold group (PL 977), circa 1959—sleek T-Rex, Brontosaurus, Trachodon, Dimetrodon, Triceratops, Ankylosaurus, Stegosaurus, Allosaurus.

5. Second Series mold group (PL1083), circa 1961—Megatherium, Mammoth, Moschops, Styrachosaurus, Iguanodon, Parasaurolophus, Struthiomimus, Smilodon.

Marx dinosaurs, some believe, were first produced in the early to mid-1950s. In actuality, production couldn't be verified until 1955-1956. The original Marx line consisted of fourteen dinosaur pieces from mold groups PL749, PL750, and PL755. These pieces were released in stores, and sold loosely in store bins and as bagged sets during the late 1950s. These figures were made exclusively, in that time period, in gray and green colors only, and were produced in the classic Marx lead-based soft plastic. The figures sold from 10¢ to 25¢ each, and the success of these sales prompted Marx to release its first prehistoric playset in 1957.

The original Marx playset consisted of all fourteen original dinosaurs, plus multiples of the small mold group (three extra Dimetrodons, three extra Plateosaurs, and one extra Triceratops, Sphenacodon, and Cynognathus). This totals twenty-three dinosaurs in all.

For the most part, these playset dinosaurs came exclusively in gray and green. However, Marx would occasionally revel in producing one of the large mold PL749 pieces in a metallic green or metallic silver color. Generally, only one of these brilliant-colored pieces was found in a playset. And, it was considered the true gem of the lot. The first playset, numbered #3390 and labeled "The Prehistoric Times Playset, Series 1000," also included a large vacuform mountain lake, along with twelve cavemen (six tan and six cream-colored, although they sometimes showed up in brick red and gray), four trees, four ferns, two dead tree stumps, a dead tree, and the Marx booklet. The stylish lithographed box measures

Fig. M-2: Marx carded dinosaurs, circa 1950s

16 x 27 inches, and two variations are known to exist—one with fold-in flaps, and one with a carrying case handle. This is the set most people remember from their childhood, and the set most strive to recapture. My experiences show that most Marx collectors have a vivid recollection of the fragile vacuform lake. This single-piece scenery formation is quite large (box-sized) and has smoothly contoured hills and a waterfall. Because of its brittle quality (it has the consistency of a Halloween mask), it tended to crack easily. Therefore, most often, the vacuform was the first part of the set to be discarded. Because of this, finding a #3390 playset with a mint condition vacuform lake, now more than forty years old, is rare. The other tough-to-find and highly desirable piece of this playset is the Marx booklet, with drawings and descriptions of the animals.

For the cost-conscious dinosaur fan, Marx issued small, modified versions of its playsets in the late

Fig. M-3: Marx second series blister card from the late 1960s, with two tan plastic items

1950s, as well. Usually packaged in a small polka-dot box, the mini-playsets were known to contain about thirteen dinosaurs and three cavemen, without all the other glorious playset accessories. These mini-sets are now even rarer than the full boxed versions.

The #3390 Marx set, along with most other playset formats, came packaged in a variety of numbers. The reasons for this are unknown, but many have speculated that it had to do with the number of pieces in the sets, or even for purposes of where the sets were marketed. I have an unnumbered #3388 set with a sticker on the back claiming it to be a Montgomery Ward exclusive. The #3389 set came in the large 16 x 27-inch box as well, but it is totally devoid of any box art. It is packaged in an antique-looking plain brown box, with only the words "Marx Prehistoric Playset, Series 500" on the cover. I have been told by many Marx enthusiasts that the plain box sets were released through retail outlets like Sears and Montgomery Wards by mail-order only. The box art sets were sold through the stores themselves. This is a fact I cannot verify, but it sounds plausible. The significance of the series number is also a mystery. The #3392 playset, I believe, has fewer dinosaurs, although the set is identical in most other respects.

In mid-1958, riding the wave of success of the #3390 playset, Marx produced and released another playset, Prehistoric Times #3388, although it was also released as the #3394 set, and even sometimes came unnumbered altogether. This set was packaged in a small lithographed 18 x 15-inch box. This box, too, had a beautiful lithograph depicting a Brontosaurus in the foreground, and a Pot-Bellied T-Rex in the background eating a Plateosaurus. The shadowy silhouette of a Kronosaurus adorns the front left of the box. This set contains (usually) thirty-one dinosaurs (generally one PL749, two PL750, and two PL755, plus two sleek T-Rexes.) Many collectors, however, have told me they have totally different dinosaur contents in this set, and some even claim to have the revised PL977 mold group included. Apparently, Marx had no standards for what actually went into a playset, other than that it contain a certain predetermined number of pieces, be they animal or accessory.

The biggest addition to this #3388 set was a new T-Rex (the sleek, revised version) which accompanied the Pot-Bellied Rex in this set. The sleek T-Rex was a much more scientifically accurate depiction of the creature by physical stature. Most sets generally contained doubles of the awesome, new, revised T-Rex, although I have seen a few that had doubles of the Pot-Belly, instead. In either case, both meat-eaters were present in this playset.

The complement of the other dinosaurs generally remained the same as in the #3390 set, but additionally included a duplicate set of the PL750 mold group in a different color.

Other notable changes in this set included the fragile vacuform plastic mountain base which was now colored in gray or brown, or marbled gray and/or brown. The trees and ferns remained constant in number, but this and subsequent Marx sets did not contain the dead tree and stumps. Additionally, this set, more often than not and for whatever reason, had no cavemen, although there have been original sets found that did have some cavemen included. One of the biggest changes in this set was in dinosaur color. Brown was introduced as a standard Marx color, and generally the PL755 mold group came in brown in this set. In addition, as is often found in the #3390 set, one or more of the large mold pieces in this set are generally in a metallic silver color, and sometimes in the rare metallic green.

A brief note here about coloring. Marx generally stood by its standard colors in initial production. Browns, grays, and greens were most common, and the aforementioned metallic green and silver were often the lone prize in the Cracker Jack (or should I say Prehistoric) box. However, the variances in color could be substantial. The brown color had a wide latitude in shading, ranging from flat, candy-bar-colored brown to deep dark brown, and even a reddish brown. On rare occasion, Marx would drizzle some color into their gray dinosaurs and make a beautiful set of swirled or marbled pieces. These are quite rare today, especially those pieces with intense marbling. What makes these pieces so desirable is that each one is unique. The marbling differs in degrees of intensity in every piece, and even the base color can differ from light gray to dark gray. I have even come across a few green pieces that have been marbled. The marbled pieces seem to have been produced mainly in the PL755 mold, and often in the PL749 mold. Marbled pieces from the PL750 mold, or the subsequent PL977 and PL1083 blister card pieces, seem to be much more rare.

Marx released a bevy of playsets during subsequent years, with different production numbers, but all were a variation of these two aforementioned sets in most respects. At the same time, Marx continued its sales of individual dinosaurs in stores. But, now they were sold in shades of brown, gray, and green. The original large mold metallic green and silver pieces were never sold as individual pieces. These were playset premium pieces only, and today are quite rare. When Marx introduced the sleek T-Rex in 1960, they produced an entirely new mold group of dinosaurs (the revised mold PL977). With the exception of the sleek Rex, all other dinosaurs are the same as their original brethren, with minor exceptions. Why Marx re-tooled the same figures has been the cause of much speculation, but most believe it was to improve the posture of the figures in some cases and, in others, simply to save on plastic. Neither of these reasons really makes a lot of sense. Why not just make an entire new set of unique animals, like they did with the PL-1083 group? Why reproduce the same figures in minutely changed form? How much plastic would really be saved? But, for want of a better reason(s), there is nothing else to account for this minor reworking of the standards.

Descriptions of the mold "revisions" and their identifying marks follow:

1. T-Rex

This is the easiest revision because the dinosaur is in a completely different pose. The original T-Rex is fondly known as the Pot-Bellied T-Rex because of his robust stomach. The sleek T-Rex, or "revised" Tyrannosaurus Rex, is more in tune with the scientific vision of what we today know a T-Rex looks like, and this figure is substantially more animated than his pot-bellied brother.

2. Brontosaurus

The original Brontosaurus is nearly identical to the revision. The original piece has four large mold circles on its feet, and the descriptive words on the animal are large, crisp, and slightly further down on the abdomen. All revised Brontos have small mold circles on their feet, and the descriptive words are small. This, and most revised mold pieces, have a slightly shinier texture, as well.

3. Trachodon

Original Trachodons have their forepaw pointing downward. This piece is slightly unbalanced and tends to lean to the left. Revised Trachodons are perfectly balanced, and the forepaw extends upward.

4. Stegosaurus

Original Stegos have a single large mold circle on the left foot. The other three feet have small mold circles. The revisions have a small mold circle on all four feet, or, in some instances, no mold circles at all.

5. Ankylosaurus

The revised Anky is slightly slimmer and has smaller legs, but the easiest way to discern the pieces is by looking at the underbelly—originals have a pebbly texture and revisions have a grid-like pattern.

6. Triceratops

Again, the revision is slightly smaller in girth, but original Trikes have thicker and firmer horns. The revision has flimsy, thin horns.

7. Allosaurus

The revised Allo has his paws tucked further under than the originals. Also, all Allosaur originals lean left in an unbalanced posture. The revisions have perfect balance, and all toes on the feet point straight forward.

8. Dimetrodon

The only visible difference in these two is that the revised Dimetrodons do not have a mold circle on their underbelly. All originals have a faint mold circle on the underbelly.

These eight figures were only known to be sold as a group on blister cards called "Prehistoric Monsters" or "Prehistoric Monsters and Cavemen," sometimes having two cavemen included on the card. They were also included in the #3398 playset. With the advent of the "revised" group of eight, Marx then took the original large mold group (PL-749) out of production. The reason for this is unknown and remains a mystery to this day. Speculation is that they simply wanted to ensure the success of the new T-Rex model. But, at the same time, they were perhaps removing (at least by today's standards for demand) their most popular creatures, in the form of the Kronosaurus and Pot-Bellied T-Rex. Because of this marketing ploy, the Pot-Belly Rex and Kronosaurus tend to be fewer in number and, therefore, in higher demand than most other Marx models. And, they exist in less diversity of color.

The eight revised pieces, on the other hand, seem to be the most common of the Marx original figures, since they were sold in abundant quantities during the period of Marx's peak popularity. Plus, it was probably more thrifty to buy a set of eight pieces together than pick them out one at a time, especially since most folks, I assume, would have wanted the new T-Rex.

There is, additionally, one addendum to the blister pack PL-977 mold story. The sleek T-Rex, being the highlight figure of the group, was released, apparently, at least two years before its remaining mold mates. And, unlike the other revised pieces, it appears to have been released in the late 1950s and sold individually, along with the other Marx original mold pieces, in store bins. I have talked to many Marx collectors who, like myself, share that recollection. We can only assume from these remembrances that the sleek Rex was originally tooled on its own mold and produced in great quantity. Its success probably prompted the production and marketing of the entire revised PL-977 mold, and the blister card sets.

In 1960-1961, Marx also released a second set of blister-carded figures. These are known as the second series pieces (PL-1083), and they came carded as a group entitled "Monsters and Mammals." The advent of this set of eight brought on the addition of yet another standard, but less common, Marx dinosaur color: tan. These pieces can often be found in the very desirable tan color on the blister cards. It is believed that pieces in the second series carded sets were never sold as individuals, but only as a carded set or as a part of the #3398 playset mentioned below.

On the heels of the PL-1083 production, in 1962-1963 Marx released the kingpin of all playsets. The #3398 Prehistoric Times Playset includes all Marx dinosaurs and cavemen except the original large mold group (PL-749). There are fifty-seven total pieces in this set, thirty-six of which are dinosaur pieces (one PL-750, two PL-755, one PL-977 and one PL-1083). This is probably the most rare and most desirable set to seek and find among collectors today. A major change in marketing strategy included the addition of a new interlocking three-piece mountain-lake set with land bridge (which came in brown or marbled brown), twelve cavemen (six tan and six cream), all the trees and ferns, and a new revised booklet. The large 12 x 24-inch box depicts the revised T-Rex walking through a time tunnel of concentric circles. The box alone is the quest of many a collector. The #3398 set usually contained the medium mold group in the very desirable tan or chocolate-milk brown colors. This is an extremely rare set of pieces in either color shade. The second series (PL-1083) figures were usually a reddish-brown color in this set. This is the only Marx playset to contain the second series pieces and the revised mold pieces, combined. This set represents the pinnacle of Marx production.

Shortly thereafter, it was believed, the U.S. government mandated that the lead pigment be removed from the paints in the Marx plastic, resulting in an inferior plastic. Subsequent stories from Marx workers seem to rebut the pigment theory, but for whatever reason, Marx dinosaur production ceased in 1964, and Marx mysteriously dropped out of the dinosaur production business. The reasons remain a mystery, but one can only assume that interest had waned somewhat and profits had plummeted. The sheer rarity of the original #3398 playset is probably a testament to that assumption. And, for whatever reason, Marx molded or produced no "new" dinosaurs or prehistoric playsets from 1964 to 1971. We can only speculate about the severity of the government mandate, but it seems that Marx was allowed to clear out its existing stock. Many collectors recall still buying Marx originals and blister card sets into the mid-1960s. We, again, can only assume that these were either existing stock from Marx inventories, or existing stock that stores still had on hand from the production era. So, although Marx was no longer producing, it is safe to say they were still selling pre-1963 production pieces at least until 1966-1967 . . . or until existing production stock was depleted.

Marx did begin reproducing dinosaurs and prehistoric playsets in 1971. The dinosaurs of the new era were the same as those that have been discussed up to this point, with one major change: Yes, the plastic was, indeed, different. Gone was the lead pigment. In its place was a waxy type of plastic that lacked the charm (and smell) as the lead-paint originals.

One of the glaring consistencies of the 1970s production was the monotony of color. The grays were all identical, as were the greens. No variation. No charm. The playsets remained popular, but to those who had possessed "originals," it was just not the same. Ironically, some of the late 1970s playsets are also some of the most rare. The Giant Prehistoric Mountain set is nearly impossible to locate in complete form these days, as is the *One Million B.C.* set. Why this is so, one can only speculate, but it soon became evident that the Marx dinosaur era had gone the way of, well . . . the way of the dinosaur.

Original Marx dinosaurs remain in great demand even today. These are the collectibles by which most other modern day models are judged. Collecting Marx is considered by some to be an art form, and is usually done by first acquiring complete sets and then, after that achievement, seeking pieces with matching colors. Most Marx fanatics look to color as a priority for collecting. Rediscovering a childhood playset in acceptable condition is a crowning achievement in collecting. Collecting color-matched Marx sets is the passion!

When attempting to color-match Marx models, it is important to keep in mind how extremely difficult this task can be. Remember, the Marx dinosaurs were produced by mold groupings, as outlined previously. So, the mold-mated dinosaurs *must* be consistent in color. In other words, if just one piece of a particular mold is found in a certain color, then all items from that mold will exist in that same color. Because the dinosaurs were produced on five different molds, color-matching them perfectly is a challenge. The only way to really ensure perfect color-matching is to find the mold grouping pieces in a playset. This bit of knowledge can come in real handy when trying to determine if the playset you've found is genuine. If it is, the dinosaur colors of the mold mates should be identical in color. If they aren't, and even if there's just a slight variation in color tone, that's a good sign that someone has thrown the set together from individual pieces, which tended to vary in shade. The sole exception to this rule is the large mold group: PL-749 was usually mixed in color, probably because they often threw one of the gem-like metallic pieces in with the group.

In Marx plastic figures, the standard green, gray, and brown color shows a wide but subtle range in variance. Additionally, it is important to note that not all Marx dinosaurs were produced in every available color.

Here, based on my experience, is a brief overview of what exists in Marx colors by mold group:

Large Mold Group (PL-749): Most common color is gray, but also abundant in green. This group was never molded in basic and darker brown colors, but is the only group to exist in silver. Also, this group was molded in a very light shade of chocolate-milk brown, but this version is extremely rare as are the marbled shades. PL-749 items were never made in tan, but they do appear in metallic green in scarce numbers.

Medium Mold Group (PL-750): Common colors again are grays and greens. This group was also never done in basic and dark brown, but does exist in rare numbers in the chocolate-milk brown and marbled tones. This group was also made in tan, in the #3398 playset only, and this is a premium and highly sought-after color. PL-750 items were never made in metallic green or silver.

Small Mold Group (PL-755): Most common color is standard green (and shades thereof). Also abundant in grays, and available in lesser numbers in browns and marbled. Never made in tan or metallic green or silver.

Revised Mold (PL-977): Used almost every Marx color with equal frequency in the grays, greens, and browns. Extremely rare in metallic green, and is also rumored to exist in tan (but I've never seen a tan piece from this group). Occasionally marbled, but never made in silver.

Second Series (PL-1083): This group was made in most colors, including different shades of tan. This group even exists in a slightly different shade of metallic green. This metallic is different than the metallic green from the PL-749 mold. The PL-749 metallic green is much more intense and brilliant. The PL-1083 metallic is a somewhat shallower color, but no less desirable. The most common colors of this mold group are brown, gray, and the various tans. I find that standard green is the least common color of this group, and borders on being rare. Made very infrequently in a very lightly swirled black on gray, but never made in silver.

Keep in mind that this discussion relates to the standard colors Louis Marx permitted for the production of his dinosaur models. Many hours were spent determining which colors kids would find desirable. It appears the Marx philosophy was based on a somewhat conservative approach—sticking with earthier tones in their original figures. But one of the critical things that made Marx so popular, besides the color of the figures, was the overall quality of its product. Unlike MPC, Timmee, Palmer, Ajax, and most other plastics dealers of the era, Marx adhered to very strict standards of quality control and production. But, one of the results of this stern insistence on top-notch productivity was an abundance of rejected raw materials.

Marx plastic dinosaurs and other figures were produced in injection molding machines. These machines, apparently, were not able to effectively use recycled plastic, so virgin plastic had to be used for each and every run of figures. Recycling was simply not an option. Any plastic pieces that did not meet pre-set standards, be it due to mis-molding, short-molding, or even color disparaging, had to be thrown out according to the Louis Marx guidelines. Needless to say, over the many, many years that Marx was in business, a staggering stash of trashed plastic items was created. So, what did Marx do to dispose of this stuff? This question has an intriguing answer.

Marx did not burn its plastic residue—they simply buried it in the now infamous Marx Toy Dump. Located about 20 miles outside of Moundsville, West Virginia, this large landfill area is (was) the final home for a glorious array of discarded Marx toys. Now, keep in mind, we're not only talking dinosaurs, we're talking every Marx plastic mold ever produced. Daily, thousands and thousands of pieces were discarded, dumped, buried, and covered over. But, as long as Marx was in business, the dump was a moot area. Owned and operated by the Marx Toy company, it was off-limits to outsiders. When Marx went out of business in the late 1970s, so did the reluctance to take up pick and shovel and visit the great plastic graveyard. Engaging in a paleontological dig was no longer limited to certified paleontologists with a true fossil mission. The collector, with his own passion and appreciation for "fossil toys," could pursue his own dig. But, as in real life fossil hunting, this, in most cases, might very well be a fruitless venture. The Marx landfill area occupies an expansive tract of land, and actually finding a dumped area is somewhat akin to finding a T-Rex fossil lying openly in a desert bed of sand. Nevertheless, humans—and especially toy collectors—are, as we know, quite obsessive. What lies below those grounds in West Virginia was, and is, a mystery, and we all know that human beings love a good mystery. A few failures never dissuaded any passionate toy collector. A trip to the Marx dump can be quite a revealing experience.

Although located on what are now public lands, the dump is only accessible by passing through private properties. Landowners in the area are keenly aware of the curious nature of this property, so passage and entry is no easy task. Most landowners are alert and on guard for any passersby. It takes quite a stipend to gain entry, but if you are one of the lucky few who can gain legal access, and if you are among the lucky few who knows just where to dig, a mother lode could result from the effort.

Found in the dump in recent years have been not-so-prehistoric dinosaurs of the most unusual and glorious color. To collectors they are gold. Obsessive "Marxists" thinking that they had already collected all that existed in the Marx dinosaur family were introduced to an entire new realm of color. We had to start all over! The gold rush was on!

Of course, not all were and are gems. Among the items uncovered were the usual complement of mold mishaps . . . prehistoric thalidomide creatures attached at the chest, or with legs and arms missing; and ink-spotted pieces or items with tails that were short molded. In fact, as you might expect, the first foot or two of digging reveals plastics that are rendered virtually useless by the effects of weathering and the elements of nature. Deeper down, however, are the "prehistoric" treasures. Untouched and often pristine pieces have been found which were discarded simply because of color. Beautiful robin's egg blue pieces have been found in abundance in absolutely mint condition. The more moody moss-green shades are plentiful, and the combo shades that resulted from paint mixing are overwhelming. Brownish grays, grayish greens, muddy browns, and

brown-like tans lie buried, in addition to a variety of multi-colored pieces. All of these are presumably the result of a color change in molding, or perhaps even some creative experimenting by Marx staff. All of these, for whatever reason, were relegated to the trash heap in the 1960s. But, as they say, one man's garbage in 1960 is another man's gold in 1999!

What does all this mean? Perhaps nothing . . . unless you are a completist like most avid Marx collectors. This seems to be a trait all erstwhile collectors share. We can never get enough where Marx is concerned, and although some may believe this hobby to be frivolous and stupid, to Marx fanatics it is a rekindling of the creative and inquisitive spirit we had as kids. Each Marx model, in its own right, conjures up memories from a treasured childhood experience. Each piece has its own charm and unique place in our collective lives. The leaded plastic has a distinctive odor that devoted Marx collectors find intoxicating. Each dinosaur and every different color has its own special meaning to remind us of where we were, or what we were doing at some precise time in our long-ago past. And, for that reason, the spirit of childhood, and of recapturing our youth, is forever linked to these glorious models of our youth—the foundation that made us all what we are today.

MARX PLASTIC FIGURES AND PLAYSETS VALUE GUIDE
(Figs. M-1 - M-3)

Allosaurus, 60 mm $7-12
Ankylosaurus, 60 mm 7-12
Brontosaurus, 60 mm (fig. M-4) 10-15
Caveman holding rock over head, 6", 1960s
    (fig. M-5) 3-6
Caveman holding rock over head, 45 mm,
    cream or tan (fig. M-6) 3-4
Caveman holding rock over head, 45 mm,
    gray or brick red 5-8
Caveman running with club, knife, 6", 1960s
    (fig. M-7) 3-6
Caveman running with stone ax, 6", 1960s
    (fig. M-8) 3-6
Caveman standing, one foot forward, 6",
    1960s 3-6
Caveman with club, knife, 45 mm, cream
    or tan (fig. M-9) 3-4
Caveman with rock, flint, 45 mm, cream
    or tan (fig. M-10) 3-4
Caveman walking with club, 45 mm, cream
    or tan (fig. M-11) 3-4

Fig. M-4: Brontosaurus

Caveman walking with club, 45 mm, gray
    or brick red 5-8
Caveman wielding club, 6", 1960s (fig. M-12) . 3-6
Caveman with club, knife, 45 mm, gray or
    brick red $5-8
Caveman with rock, flint, 45 mm, gray or
    brick red 5-8
Caveman standing with spear, 45 mm, cream
    or tan (fig. M-13) 3-4
Caveman skinning rabbit, 45 mm, cream
    or tan (fig. M-14) 3-4
Caveman skinning rabbit, 45 mm, gray or
    brick red 5-8

Fig. M-5: Caveman holding rock over head, 6"

Fig. M-6: Caveman holding rock over head, 45 mm

Fig. M-7: Caveman running with club and knife

Fig. M-8: Caveman running with stone ax

Fig. M-9: Caveman with club and knife

Fig. M-10: Caveman with rock and flint

Fig. M-11: Caveman walking with club

Fig. M-12: Caveman wielding club

Fig. M-13: Caveman standing with spear

Fig. M-14: Caveman skinning rabbit

Fig. M-15: Caveman squatting with spear

Fig. M-20: Moschops

Fig. M-19: Megatherium

Fig. M-22: Stegosaurus   **Fig. M-21:** Pteranodon

Fig. M-16: Cynognathus

Fig. M-17: Iguanodon

Fig. M-23: Triceratops

Fig. M-18: Kronosaurus

Woolly Mammoth, 60 mm (fig. M-25) 10-15
Metallic Green Figure, any animal
(fig. M-26). $40-60
Metallic Silver Figure, any animal 20-25
Tan figure, any animal 20-25

Playsets

#3390 1957 Prehistoric Times
(fig. M-27) $200-350
#3391 1958 Prehistoric (small set) 50-100
#3389 1957 Prehistoric 200-300
#3388 1958 Prehistoric Times. 275-350
#3393 1959 Prehistoric 200-250
#3394 1959 Prehistoric 200-250
#3397 1960 Prehistoric Times (fig. M-28) 100-200
#2650 1961 Prehistoric (small set,
rare box) 190-240
#3392 1961 Prehistoric Times. 200-300
#0645 1962 Prehistoric 125-200
#3375 1962 Prehistoric 150-250
#3398 1963 Prehistoric Times (fig. M-29) 400-500
#3398 1970 Prehistoric Times. 100-150
#3421 1974 One Million B.C. 175-250
#3414 1975 Prehistoric Mountain 175-250

#4304 1977 Giant Prehistoric Mountain 175-250
#4208 1978 Prehistoric Dinosaur
(fig. M-30) $50-75
#4209 1978 Prehistoric Dinosaur
(smaller box) 50-75
#4130 1979 World of Dinosaurs
(fig. M-31) 100-150
Sears Exclusive, Prehistoric Animals and
Cavemen, 16 pieces, polka-dot box
(fig. M-32) 90-120
Sears Exclusive, Prehistoric Animal Set,
13 pieces, polka-dot box 80-110

Fig. M-25: Woolly Mammoth

Fig. M-26: Metallic Green Figures

Fig. M-24: Tyrannosaurus

Fig. M-27: Prehistoric Times playset, 1957

Fig. M-30: Prehistoric Dinosaur playset, 1978

Fig. M-28: Prehistoric Times playset, 1960

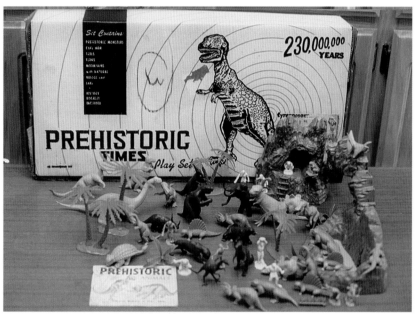

Fig. M-29: Prehistoric Times playset, 1963

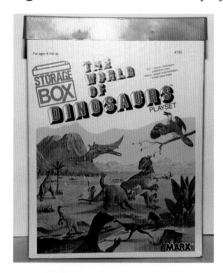

Fig. M-31: World of Dinosaurs playset, 1979

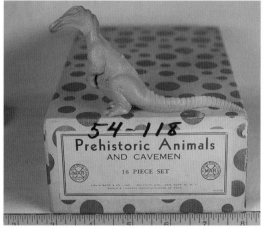

Fig. M-32: Sears Exclusive—Prehistoric Animals and Cavemen

Fig. 2-1: Brontosaurus

METAL FIGURES

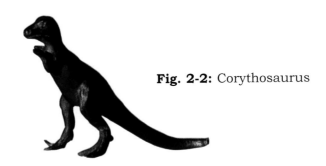

Fig. 2-2: Corythosaurus

ALVA

In the 1950s, Alva released a line of metal dinosaur figures, now highly sought by collectors.

Brontosaurus (fig. 2-1) $100-150
Corythosaurus (fig. 2-2) 100-150
Plateosaurus (fig. 2-3) 100-150
Stegosaurus (fig. 2-3) 100-150
Trachodon (fig. 2-3) 100-150
Tyrannosaurus 100-150

Fig. 2-3: Plateosaurus, Trachodon, Stegosaurus

CUTERI

Cuteri's pewter prehistoric animals average from 1.5 to 2 inches in length.

Brontosaurus, 2" $7-12
Dimetrodon, 1.75" 7-12
Mammoth, 1" 7-12
Stegosaurus, 1.75" 7-12
Triceratops, (frill curls, like a wave) 1.75" . . 7-12
Tyrannosaurus, 1.5" 7-12

DINO LAND BRASS

Based in White Post, Virginia, Dino Land issued a small series of hollow polished-brass dinosaurs, each 5-6 inches long.

Ceratosaurus $7-10
Stegosaurus 7-10
Triceratops 7-10

FRANKLIN MINT
(See Chapter 3—Ceramic and Resin Figures.)

Fig. 2-4: Brontosaurus

Fig. 2-8: Protoceratops with nest (original version)

Fig. 2-9: Stegosaurus

Fig. 2-5: Mammoth

Fig. 2-6: Scelidosaurus

Fig. 2-10: Triceratops

Fig. 2-11: Parasauralophus

Fig. 2-12: Edaphosaurus

Fig. 2-7: Tyrannosaurus

FUNRISE DIECAST

In 1988, Funrise produced several toy dinosaurs in plastic and diecast. The company's diecast dinosaurs were sold on individual blister packs with collector cards. Each is 2-3 inches long.

Brachiosaurus $5-8
Brontosaurus (fig. 2-4) 5-8
Iguanodon 5-8
Mammoth (fig. 2-5) 5-8
Scelidosaurus (fig. 2-6) 5-8
Stegosaurus 5-8
Triceratops 5-8
Tyrannosaurus (fig. 2-7) 5-8

GRENADIER

These metal miniatures were originally issued in two sets of four in 1982. The Protoceratops was originally packaged with a nest, which was later discontinued.

Set 1: Tyrannosaurus, Ankylosaurus,
  Protoceratops, Dimetrodon, painted
  metal $10-15
Set 1: Original version with Protoceratops
  nest (fig. 2-8) 25-35
Set 2: Stegosaurus, Triceratops,
  Parasauralophus, Edaphosaurus,
  painted metal (figs. 2-9 to 2-12) 10-15
Raptor Rider War Leader, unpainted
  pewter, gaming piece pack, 1992 8-12

H.S. BRUMM FLAT METAL

Produced in Germany, these delicate silvery pieces are flat, and are embossed differently on each side. The original molds are believed to date back to the early 1900s, and the pieces were cast, off and on, until about the 1950s, when it is believed the last castings were made. The pieces were produced in conjunction with Germany's Flat Metal Society, a

Fig. 2-13: Ankylosaurus

Fig. 2-16: Dimetrodon

Fig. 2-19: Megatherium with tree

Fig. 2-14: Coelodonta

Fig. 2-17: Diplodocus

Fig. 2-15: Crocodile with small dinosaur

Fig. 2-18: Duckbill

Fig. 2-20: Pterodactyl perched on rock

group primarily involved with military pieces, so the dinosaurs were largely ignored until they were "rediscovered" fairly recently. Brumm flat metal pieces have never been made commercially available through normal retail outlets, and not many sets were produced, so they are tough to obtain.

The original set included forty-six pieces—thirty-six dinosaurs and ten plants and trees. Later, several prehistoric mammals were added, bringing the total set up to sixty-eight pieces. Also included with the set is a poster showing the original forty-six pieces. The figures were originally intended to be cleaned-up and painted, a common hobby among flat metal enthusiasts. However, because this prehistoric series is so finely crafted and detailed, few are willing to risk painting the items.

Fig. 2-21: Scelidosaurus

Fig. 2-22: Leaping Smilodon

Ankylosaurus (fig. 2-13) $20-30
Coelodonta (rhino) (fig. 2-14) 30-50
Crocodile with small dinosaur (fig. 2-15) . . 30-50
Dimetrodon (fig. 2-16) 30-50
Diplodocus (fig. 2-17) 30-50
Duckbill (fig. 2-18) 30-50
Megatherium (Sloth) with tree (fig. 2-19) . . 30-50

Pterodactyl perched on rock (fig. 2-20) . . $30-50
Scelidosaurus (fig. 2-21) 20-30
Smilodon leaping (Saber-Toothed Tiger)
  (fig. 2-22) 30-50

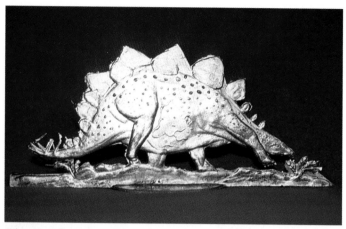
Fig. 2-23: Stegosaurus

Fig. 2-24: Styracosaurus

Fig. 2-25: Tyrannosaurus eating

Fig. 2-26: Water fight between Plesiosaurus and foe

Fig. 2-27: Woolly Mammoth head and Caveman

Stegosaurus (fig. 2-23) $30-50
Styracosaurus (fig. 2-24) 30-50
Trees or plants, each 10-20
Tyrannosaurus eating (fig. 2-25) 30-50
Water Fight (Plesiosaurus and foe)
    (fig. 2-26) 30-50
Woolly Mammoth head and Caveman
    (fig. 2-27) 30-50

Full set of 68 pieces with poster 750-1000

HUGH ROSE STUDIOS

This studio issued a line of bronze dinosaurs in 1987, available individually or as a subscription series. Sculpted by Doris Tischler, these figures are certainly among the priciest of all dinosaur collectibles.

Allosaurus vs. Stegosaurus, 1/50
    scale, limited edition of 65 . . . $1,200-1,300
Ankylosaurus vs. Albertosaurus,
    1/50 scale, limited edition of 65   1,200-1,300
Brachiosaurus, 1/50 scale, limited
    edition of 65 1,100-1,200
Dimetrodon and Edaphosaurus,
    1/25 scale, limited edition of 65   1,200-1,300
Hydrotherosaurus, 1/50 scale,
    limited edition of 50 950-1050
Pachycephalosauruses, 1/50 scale,
    limited edition of 65 1,200-1,300
Parasaurolophus vs. Dromaeosaurs,
    1/50 scale, limited edition of 50 . 1,200-1,300
Pteranodon vs. Tylosaurus,
    1/50 scale, limited edition of 50 . . . 900-1000
Triceratops mother and baby,
    1/50 scale, limited edition of 50 . . . 900-1000
Tyrannosaurus, 1/50 scale, limited
    edition of 50 900-1000

Silver Jewelry Pieces, sold and given free to subscribers, by Jim Morris Jewelers, Curville, TX

Jewelry Piece, Deinonychus, 1/50 scale,
    sterling silver $35-50
Jewelry Piece, Ornitholestes eating
    Archaeopteryx, 1/50 scale,
    sterling silver 40-60

LANCE PEWTER
See Miller Enterprises.

Fig. 2-28: Mignot dinosaur figures

Fig. 2-29: Plesiosaur

LOS ANGELES MUSEUM OF NATURAL HISTORY

In the late 1960s, the Los Angeles Museum of Natural History issued a line of heavy brass prehistoric mammal figures, each about 5-6" long.

Arctodus	$100-150
Bison	100-150
Cave Bear	100-150
Cave Lion	100-150
Dinohyus	100-150
Dire Wolf	100-150
Glossotherium	100-150
Imperial Mammoth	100-150
Mesohippus	100-150
Smilodon	100-150
Teratornis	100-150

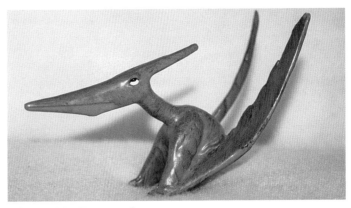

Fig. 2-30: Pteranodon

MIGNOT

This French company traces its origins back to 1785, and is best known for producing toy soldiers. Early in this century, possibly in the 1920s, Mignot began producing its dinosaur line, which is still in production today. The figures are heavy, made of a cast lead/tin/antimony alloy. (Fig. 2-28)

Fig. 2-31: Triceratops

Diplodocus, 16" long	$100-120
Mastodon, 4"	100-120
Mushroom, 2.25"	50-75
Mushroom, 4.25"	50-75
Plesiosaur, 6" long (fig. 2-29)	100-120
Pteranodon, 3" (fig. 2-30)	70-90
Thylosaur, 6"	70-90
Tree, prehistoric palm, 6.5"	50-75
Triceratops, 7" (fig. 2-31)	100-120

Fig. 2-32: Allosaurus

MILLER ENTERPRISES (LANCE PEWTER)

In the early 1990s, paleontologist Wade Miller teamed with artist Gary Ginther to create a line of pewter and limited edition bronze dinosaurs. The pieces were sold through the Earth Sciences Museum in Provo, Utah, and are now also available directly from Miller Enterprises. Six figures were released in 1993, in both pewter and bronze versions. In 1995, three more pewter figures were introduced. At press time, it was believed that three more pewter figures would be released soon, bringing the company's line up to an even dozen dinosaurs. All are built to 1/80 scale.

Pewter Figures

Allosaurus, 3", 1993 (fig. 2-32) $35-45
Ceratosaurus, 2.5", 1993 (fig. 2-33) 30-40
Stegosaurus, 4" long, 1993 (fig. 2-34) 30-40
Supersaurus, 15" long, 1993 (fig. 2-35) . 85-115
Torvosaurus, 3", 1993 (fig. 2-36) 30-40
Triceratops, 4" long, 1995 (fig. 2-37) 40-50
Tyrannosaurus, 6" long, 1995 (fig. 2-38) . . 60-75
Ultrasaurus, 8.5", 1993 (fig. 2-39) 100-150
Utahraptor, 3", 1995 (fig. 2-40) 35-50
Full set of 9 figures 325-400

Fig. 2-33: Ceratosaurus

Fig. 2-34: Stegosaurus

Fig. 2-35: Supersaurus

Fig. 2-36: Torvosaurus

Fig. 2-37: Triceratops

Fig. 2-39: Ultrasaurus

Fig. 2-38: Tyrannosaurus

Fig. 2-40: Utahraptor

Bronze Figures, limited editions of 100 pieces

Allosaurus, 3", 1993 . . . . $200-300
Ceratosaurus, 2.5", 1993 200-300
Stegosaurus, 4" long, 1993 200-300
Supersaurus, 15" long, 1993 350-450
Torvosaurus, 3", 1993 200-300
Ultrasaurus, 8.5", 1993 350-450
Complete set, editions 1-10, each . . 1,800-2,000
Complete set, editions 11-100, each 1,400-1,600

NOVUS ENTERPRISES

This firm released some cast iron dinosaurs in the 1990s that appear to be re-casts of Safari's Carnegie Museum pieces.

Baby Apatosaurus $7-12
Stegosaurus 7-12

PERTH PEWTER

In 1986, Perth released a set of six detailed pewter dinosaurs, averaging 4 inches in length.

Apatosaurus, 4.25" long $18-24
Pteranodon on dead tree stump, 4.5" tall . 18-24
Stegosaurus 18-24
Triceratops 18-24
Tyrannosaurus, large, 5" long 20-25
Tyrannosaurus, small 18-24
Set of 6 110-135

PEWTER IMAGES

This Sarasota, Florida-based company has issued two lines of pewter dinosaurs, both of which are still currently available.

Brontosaurus, 1.5" tall $8-12
Dimetrodon, 2.25" long 8-12
Pteranodon over wave, 2.5" 8-12
Stegosaurus, 2" 8-12
Triceratops, 3" long with long horns
   and legs 22-28
Triceratops, 1.75" 8-12
Tyrannosaurus with foot on rock, 3" 22-28
Tyrannosaurus, 2" 8-12

RADIO PREMIUMS (OG, SON OF FIRE)

In the 1930s, the radio show Og, Son of Fire produced a line of lead figure premiums, including four cave people and two dinosaurs.

Caveman, "Og," painted lead on square
   base, 1930s (fig. 2-41) $50-60
Caveman, "Big Tooth," holding bow,
   painted lead on square base,
   1930s (fig. 2-42) 50-60
Caveman running, "Ru," painted lead on
   square base, 1930s (fig. 2-43) 50-60
Cavewoman, "Nada," painted lead on
   square base, 1930s (fig. 2-44) 50-60
Dinosaur, "Fang," painted lead, 1930s . . 75-100
Dinosaur, "Rex," painted lead, 1930s . . . 75-100

Fig. 2-41: Caveman, "Og"

Fig. 2-42: Caveman, "Big Tooth"

Fig. 2-43: Caveman running, "Ru"

Fig. 2-44: Cavewoman, "Nada"

Fig. 2-45: Smilodon

Fig. 2-46: Brontosaurus

Fig. 2-47: Triceratops

RAL PARTHA (PARTHA PEWTER)

In the 1980s, Ral Partha began issuing a miniature series of raw lead and pewter dinosaurs, some aimed at the gaming market. At press time, many of the original Ral Partha and Partha Pewter pieces were about to be re-issued. Because of this re-release, pricing for these pieces may vary drastically.

Allosaurus, large size, pewter, 4" long,
1988 . . . . $15-20

Brontotherium, large size, pewter, 1988 . . 15-20

Ceratosaurus, large size, pewter, 1988 . . . 15-20

Danae with Smilodon, 3", #01714 5-8

Deinonychus (feathered), small size, 1988 . 8-12

Dicraeosaurus, large size, pewter, 5" long,
1988 15-20

Dimetrodon, small size, 1988 8-12

Dopak with Hyaenodon, 3", #01704 5-8

Erythosaurus, small size, 1988 8-12

Kala with Phorhusracus, 3", #01713 5-8

Megalosaurus, large size, pewter, 1988 . . . 15-20

Phororhacus, small size, 1988 8-12

Smilodon (Saber-Toothed Tiger), 2", #02945
(fig. 2-45) 3-5

Shona with daphoenus, 3", #01709 5-8

Sphenacodon, small size, 1988 8-12

Triceratops 18-25

Tyrannosaurus 35-45

Velociraptors (3), gaming figures, 2.5" 7-10

RAWCLIFFE PEWTER

Based in Rhode Island, Rawcliffe has issued two lines of pewter dinosaurs, and has also released some Ral Partha pewter figures. Rawcliffe's larger figures average 4-5 inches long, while its "Midget" series figures measure in at just 1.5-2.5 inches.

Brontosaurus, 5.5" long $15-20

Brontosaurus, Midget series (fig. 2-46) 5-10

Dimetrodon, 4" long $15-20

Dimetrodon, Midget series 5-10

Mammoth, Midget series 5-10

Pteranodon, Midget series 5-10

Smilodon, Midget series 5-10

Stegosaurus, 4.5" long 15-20

Stegosaurus, Midget series 5-10

Styracosaurus, 4" long 15-20

Triceratops, 4" long 15-20

Triceratops, Midget series (fig. 2-47) 5-10

Tyrannosaurus, 3" long 15-20

Tyrannosaurus, Midget series 5-10

ROYAL ONTARIO MUSEUM (BIRTHDAY SET)

Known primarily for its line of small plastic dinosaurs, the Royal Ontario Museum also produced a set of metal figural dinosaur birthday candle holders. Each has a flat base and a hole in its back. The set came packaged in a metal container with a lid that features a figural T-Rex holding up a "Happy Birthday" sign. The five dinosaurs included in the set are Stegosaurus, T-Rex, Velociraptor, Spinosaurus, and Triceratops. Each is marked "NETZKE" on the bottom.

Boxed set, 1990s $50-70

SAURIER FLAT METAL

Saurier, a company headquartered in Switzerland, produced a series of flat metal dinosaurs similar to the H.S. Brumm line, although typically smaller and requiring less clean-up to remove tiny metal burrs. This series, believed to have been produced around the 1970s, includes a total of twenty-three pieces whose molds were patterned after the paintings of Charles Knight.

Brontosaurus walking up hill (fig. 2-48) . $15-25

Ichthyosaurs (fig. 2-49) 15-25

Plesiosaurus (fig. 2-50) 15-25

Fig. 2-48: Brontosaurus walking up hill

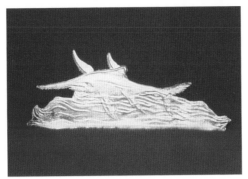

Fig. 2-49: Ichthyosaurs

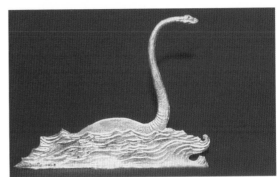

Fig. 2-50: Plesiosaurus

Fig. 2-51: Brontosaurus

Fig. 2-52: Caveman

Fig. 2-53: Dimetrodon

Fig. 2-54: Dinichthys fish

SPOONTIQUE

Spoontique released two lines of pewter dinosaur figures in the 1980s. The first series featured ten smaller pieces, measuring 2-3 inches, each with a nameplate at its base. In 1987, the firm issued several larger figures. Spoontique dinosaurs are marked with a "PP serial number" on the bottom, probably indicating a relationship with Partha Pewter.

Anatosaurus, small series, PP1079 . . . . . $25-35
Apatosaurus, small series, 3", PP1087 . . . 25-35
Apatosaurus, large series, 4", PP795 30-50
Dimetrodon, small series, PP1083 25-35
Parasauralophus, small series, ... 25-35
Plesiosaurus, small series 25-35
Pteranodon, small series, PP1085 25-35
Stegosaurus, small series, PP1084 25-35
Stegosaurus, large series, 3", PP796 30-50
Triceratops, small series, PP1086 25-35
Tyrannosaurus Rex, small series, 2",
    PP1082 25-35
Tyrannosaurus Rex, large series, 3",
    PP794 30-50
Velociraptor, small series, 2.5", PP1080 . . 25-35

SRG (SELL RITE GIFTWARE)

In the 1940s and 1950s, New York-based Sell Rite Giftware (SRG) issued a line of wonderful dinosaur figures, in two sizes. Many are marked "1947," and they are made of heavy bronze-coated lead. A plastic set, cast from the SRG molds, was released in the 1960s.

Brontosaurus, 7" long (fig. 2-51) $60-90
Brontosaurus, 4" long 35-50
Caveman, 2.75" (fig. 2-52). 35-50
Caveman, large size 60-90
Cavewoman, 2.5", ... 50-75
Cavewoman, large size 75-125
Dimetrodon, 7" long (fig. 2-53) 60-90
Dimetrodon, 4" long 35-50
Dinichthys (Dunkleoteus), fish, large size
    (fig. 2-54) 250-300
Hadrosaur, 4.25" 60-90

Fig. 2-55: Hadrosaur

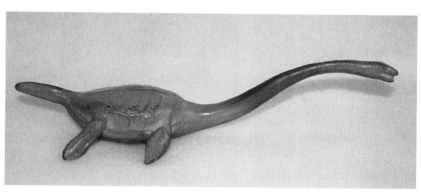

Fig. 2-57: Plesiosaur

Fig. 2-56: Mosasaurus

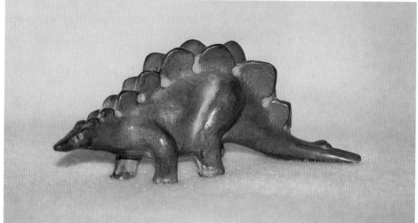

Fig. 2-58: Stegosaurus

Hadrosaur, 2.25" (fig. 2-55) $35-50
Mosasaurus, 3" long (fig. 2-56) 75-125
Mosasaurus, large size 175-225
Plesiosaur, 6.5" long (fig. 2-57) 60-90
Plesiosaur, 3.75" long 35-50
Pteranodon (Pterodactyl), 3" long 50-100
Pteranodon (Pterodactyl), large size 150-200
Stegosaurus, 5" long (fig. 2-58) 60-90
Stegosaurus, 3" long 35-50
Triceratops, 4.5" long (fig. 2-59) 60-90
Triceratops, 3.25" long 35-50
Tyrannosaurus, 3" (fig. 2-60) 60-90
Tyrannosaurus, 2" 35-50
Woolly Mammoth, large size 150-200
Woolly Mammoth, 1.5" (fig. 2-61) 50-100

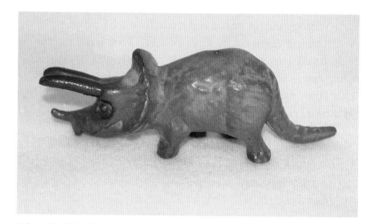

Fig. 2-59: Triceratops

SUNWEST SILVER
This Albuquerque-based firm issued a twelve-piece set of polished pewter dinosaurs in the 1980s. Each is about 1.5-2.5 inches long.

Ankylosaurus $4-8
Apatosaurus 4-8
Coelophysis 4-8
Dimetrodon 4-8

Elasmosaurus $4-8
Parasauralophus 4-8
Pteranodon on rock pile 4-8
Saber-Toothed Tiger 4-8
Stegosaurus 4-8
Triceratops 4-8
Tyrannosaurus 4-8
Woolly Mammoth 4-8

Fig. 2-60: Tyrannosaurus

Fig. 2-61: Woolly Mammoth

Fig. 2-62 (left): Cast-iron Brontosaurus
Fig. 2-62 (right): Cast-iron Smilodon

Fig. 2-63: "The Tyrant Prince," pewter T-Rex

TIMMEE TOYS

In the 1980s, Timmee issued metal versions of six of its popular vintage plastic dinosaur figures.

Brontosaurus	$2-4
Dimetrodon	2-4
Mammoth	2-4
Rhamphorhynchus	2-4
Stegosaurus	2-4
Triceratops	2-4

OTHER METAL FIGURES

Brass Brontosaurus, polished brass, 4" long, marked "hand made in India"	$8-12
Brass Stegosaurus, polished brass, 4" long, marked "hand made in India"	8-12
Brass Tyrannosaurus, polished brass, 3.5" long, marked "hand made in India"	8-12
Cast-iron Brontosaurus, 5", 1933 World's Fair, Messmore & Damon's 1 Million Years Ago (fig. 2-62, left)	100-150
Cast-iron Smilodon, 5", 1933 World's Fair, Messmore & Damon's 1 Million Years Ago (fig. 2-62, right)	100-150
Dimetrodon, heavy metal, 7" long with short sail, unmarked	40-65
"The Tyrant Prince," pewter T-Rex on wood base, Marvel comic book tie-in, Ltd. Ed., Madhouse, 1993 (fig. 2-63)	100-150

Fig. 3-2: Ankylosaurus

Fig. 3-3: Nothosaurus

Fig. 3-4: Diplodocus

CERAMIC AND RESIN FIGURES

Fig. 3-1: Abbeon ceramic dinosaurs

ABBEON

Based in Japan, Abbeon produced a line of glossy ceramic dinosaurs in the 1950s and 1960s. (fig. 3-1)

Allosaurus $50-75
Ankylosaurus (fig. 3-2) 30-50
Brontosaurus 30-50
Corythosaurus 50-75
Dimetrodon 30-50
Iguanodon 50-75
Moschops 50-75
Nothosaurus (fig. 3-3) 50-75
Parasauralophus 50-75
Pteranodon 30-50
Stegosaurus 30-50
Styracosaurus 30-50
Triceratops 30-50
Tyrannosaurus 30-50

AUS-BEN STUDIOS

This series of painted resin pieces was made in the United States in 1987. Each figure is 3-5 inches tall.

Diplodocus (fig. 3-4) $20-30

Lambeosaurus walking past tree stump
(fig. 3-5) $20-30
Plesiosaurus with marine plant base
(fig. 3-6) 20-30
Pteranodon on rock pile, dark with red eye,
5" (fig. 3-7) 20-30
Triceratops (fig. 3-8) 20-30
Tyrannosaurus running with tail out
(fig. 3-9) 20-30

Fig. 3-5: Lambeosaurus

Fig. 3-6: Plesiosaurus

Fig. 3-7: Pteranodon

AVERY CREATIONS

In 1993, Avery Creations produced a series of resin dinosaurs mimicking the "superdeformed" style popularized in Japan.

Brontosaurus, mouth open, tail up, 4.75",
   1993 (fig. 3-10) $8-12
Triceratops, mouth open, tail up, 4", 1993
   (fig. 3-11) 8-12
Tyrannosaurus, bright red open mouth, 5",
   1993 (fig. 3-12) 8-12

Fig. 3-8: Triceratops

Fig. 3-10: Brontosaurus

Fig. 3-9: Tyrannosaurus

Fig. 3-11: Triceratops

Fig. 3-12: Tyrannosaurus

BONE CHINA FAMILY MINIATURES

Several three-piece dinosaur families have been issued in bone china over the years.

Brontosaurus family, 3 pieces, 1-1.5" $5-10
Dimetrodon family, 3 pieces, 1-1.5" 5-10
Stegosaurus family, 3 pieces, 1-1.5" 5-10
Tyrannosaurus family, 3 pieces, 1-1.5"
  (fig. 3-13) 5-10

Fig. 3-13: Tyrannosaurus family

CASTAGNA

These beautifully-painted pieces are on desert-like bases, made in Italy, 1988. They are about 3-5 inches tall.

Brontosaurus (fig. 3-14) $25-40
Mammoth (fig. 3-15) 25-40
Pteranodon on rock pile (fig. 3-16) 25-40
Stegosaurus (fig. 3-17) 25-40
Triceratops (fig. 3-18) 25-40
Tyrannosaurus (fig. 3-19) 25-40

Fig. 3-17: Stegosaurus

Fig. 3-14: Brontosaurus

Fig. 3-15: Mammoth

Fig. 3-16: Pteranodon

Fig. 3-18: Triceratops

Fig. 3-19: Tyrannosaurus

CHIALU

Chialu, an Italian company, produced a highly collectible line of hand-painted composition material dinosaurs and prehistoric mammals in the 1950s. The series was patterned after the Zallinger murals published in *Life* magazine's "The World We Live In" series, originally published in 1953.

Ankylosaurus, reddish brown, no tail
    club, 5" long (fig. 3-20) $225-300
Boreostracon (Glyptodont), tan and
    brown, 5.5" long 200-250
Brachauchenius (short-necked plesiosaur),
    gray, 6" long 225-300
Brontosaurus, head and neck out of scale,
    short tail, black, 6.5" long 225-300
Diatryma, blue-gray with brown feet, red
    and white head, 5.5" tall (fig. 3-21) . . . 150-200
Dimetrodon, dark blue-gray with striped
    fin, 6" long 225-300

Kronosaurus, gray, 6" long $225-300
Megatherium, brown with red splotches,
    4" tall 200-250
Planetetherium, tan, 5.5" 200-250
Plateosaurus, blue gray with brown
    stripes, 5.5" tall 225-300
Pteranodon, flying, brown, 7" across 225-300
Sphenacodon, dark blue-gray, 6.5" long . 225-300
Stegosaurus, black with red centers on
    plates, light belly, no tail spikes,
    5" long 225-300
Triceratops, gray with metal horns,
    6.5" long (fig. 3-23) 225-300
Tyrannosaurus, dark color, 4" tall 225-300
Woolly Mammoth, black or gray with white
    metal tusks, 6.5" x 5.5" (fig. 3-22) 175-220

Fig. 3-20: Ankylosaurus

Fig. 3-21: Diatryma

Fig. 3-22: Woolly Mammoth

Fig. 3-23: Triceratops

CLIFF

These lightweight resin pieces, probably made of Hydrocal, were sold at hardware stores as garden decorations in the early 1990s.

Ankylosaurus, brownish red, 9.5" long $5-8
Parasauralophus, greenish brown, 7" tall 5-8
Tyrannosaurus holding bone, 8" tall (fig. 3-24) 5-8

CORLETT COLLECTIBLES

Also marked "Wild Things DAL," these resin figures were released in two sizes during the 1990s. Made in the United States, they measured 4-5 inches for the larger pieces, 2-4 inches for the smaller pieces.

Ankylosaurus, gray with white spikes,
    orange belly, 2" (fig. 3-25) $15-20
Brontosaurus, neck twisting backward, 5"
    (fig. 3-26) 25-40
Brontosaurus, tail curled forward, small
    version, 4" (fig. 3-27) 15-20
Parasauralophus with paw raised, 4.5"
    (fig. 3-28) 25-40
Spinosaurus, green with yellow-green
    sail back, 3.5" (fig. 3-29) 15-20
Stegosaurus with orange belly, spines, 4"
    (fig. 3-30) 25-40
Stegosaurus, blue with white spines, 2"
    (fig. 3-31) 15-20

Fig. 3-24: Tyrannosaurus

Fig. 3-25: Ankylosaurus

Fig. 3-26: Brontosaurus

Fig. 3-27: Brontosaurus

Fig. 3-28: Parasauralophus

Fig. 3-29: Spinosaurus

Fig. 3-30: Stegosaurus

Fig. 3-31: Stegosaurus

Fig. 3-32: Tyrannosaurus

Fig. 3-33: Tyrannosaurus

Fig. 3-34: Velociraptor

Tyrannosaurus, green and yellow with pink
  tongue, 5" (fig. 3-32) $25-40
Tyrannosaurus, showing white teeth, 4"
  (fig. 3-33) 15-20
Velociraptor, green with pink tongue, 3"
  (fig. 3-34) 15-20

FRANKLIN MINT

**In 1991, the Franklin Mint issued a series of
twelve prehistoric animals made of powdered
bronze and resins. The series, released in conjunction with the Academy of Natural Sciences in
Philadelphia, proved a bit tricky to obtain when
it was originally released. After a few false starts,
however, they became somewhat more available.
Today, these items are very hard to find. All are
on natural landscape-style bases.**

Apatosaurus, neck turning to look backward
  (fig. 3-35) $40-65
Cave Bear, growling on rocks (fig. 3-36) . . . 40-65
Corythosaurus, green, red and blue,
  looking backward (fig. 3-37) 40-65
Deinonychus, running (fig. 3-38) 40-65
Euoplocephalus, climbing on rocks
  (fig. 3-39) 40-65
Pteranodon, with red crest, flying over rocks
  (fig. 3-40) 40-65
Saber-Toothed Cat, growling with paw up
  (fig. 3-41) 40-65
Stegosaurus, walking down hill 40-65
Styracosaurus, with red spikes (fig. 3-42) . . 40-65
Tyrannosaurus Rex, running
  with mouth open 40-65
Woolly Mammoth, on snowy rock base
  (fig. 3-43) 40-65
Woolly Rhino, walking (fig. 3-44) 40-65

Fig. 3-36: Cave Bear

Fig. 3-35 (left): Apatosaurus

Fig. 3-37: Corythosaurus

Fig. 3-39: Euoplocephalus

Fig. 3-40: Pteranodon

Fig. 3-38: Deinonychus

Fig. 3-41: Saber-Toothed Cat

Fig. 3-42: Styracosaurus

HAGAN-RENAKER

This European ceramics company produced an extensive line of fine ceramic miniatures, most during the 1970s. Ranging from 1 to 1.5 inches tall, the line included a series of dinosaurs.

Brontosaurus, brown $8-12
Hadrosaur mom and baby (fig. 3-45) 10-15
Pterodactyl, green (fig. 3-46) 8-12
Triceratops, yellow 8-12
Tyrannosaurus mom and baby, brown
   (fig. 3-47) 10-15

Fig. 3-43: Woolly Mammoth

Fig. 3-45: Hadrosaur mom and baby

Fig. 3-46: Pterodactyl

Fig. 3-47: Tyrannosaurus mom and baby

Fig. 3-44: Woolly Rhino

HAI FENG MIN

Two series of three figures were known to be produced in this line, both cast in epoxy and painted. The first series, released in 1992, was sold in mass quantities at The Nature Store. The second series (1994), by some reports, was never seen in the U.S.

Brachiosaurus, 2nd series, 1994 (fig. 3-48) $20-30
Deinonychus, 1st series, 1992 (fig. 3-49) . . 10-15
Pachycephalosaurus, 1st series, 1992
    (fig. 3-50) 10-15
Pinacosaurus, 2nd series, 1994 20-30
Triceratops, 3.25",1st series, 1992(fig. 3-51) 10-15
Tyrannosaurus, 2nd series, 1994 20-30

Fig. 3-50: Pachycephalosaurus

Fig. 3-48: Brachiosaurus

Fig. 3-51: Triceratops

Fig. 3-49: Deinonychus

HELL CREEK CREATIONS
Sculptor Allen Debus created this line of resin figures.

Brontotherium $50-70
Dimetrodon Grandis (fig. 3-52) 50-70
Spinosaurus vs. Plesiosaur (fig. 3-53) 50-70
Tyrannosaurus Rex 50-70

Fig. 3-52: Dimetrodon Grandis

Fig. 3-53: Spinosaurus vs. Plesiosaur

JAPAN
One of the most sought-after ceramic dinosaurs is the "Howling Protoceratops," created in post-war Japan in the mid-1950s.

Protoceratops, howling position, sticker across
back, 3" long, mid-1950s (fig. 3-54) $45-60

Fig. 3-54: Protoceratops

LLADRO
Between 1994 and 1997, Lladro issued a small series of dinosaur figures, which are now discontinued and escalating in value.

Brutus, #7544, long neck and tail, standing
on hind legs, 7.25" $160-200
Rex, #7547, whimsical Tyrannosaurus, 5"
(fig. 3-55) 160-200
Rocky, #7545, with sail back and horn
on head, 4" (fig. 3-56) 140-175
Spike, #7543, whimsical Styracosaurus, 3"
(fig. 3-57) 130-160
Stretch, #7546, smiling Brontosaurus, 7.5"
(fig. 3-58) 160-200

Fig. 3-55: Rex, #7547

Fig. 3-56: Rocky, #7545

Fig. 3-57: Spike, #7543

Fig. 3-58: Stretch, #7546

Fig. 3-59: Stegosaurus

Fig. 3-60: Triceratops

LOSA ELECTRIC

These glossy ceramic figures were marked with a paper "hecho en Mexico" sticker.

Brontosaurus, brown, 3.5" long $6-10
Stegosaurus, violet with maroon plates, 3.5"
    long (fig. 3-59) 6-10
Triceratops, brown, 3.5" long (fig. 3-60) 6-10
Tyrannosaurus, green, 2.5" 6-10

SKU (BRAZILIAN CERAMICS)

The five-piece set of these Brazilian ceramics sells for about $100. Some have opalescent finishes. All are delightfully cheesy.

Brontosaurus, 6" $16-22
Parasauralophus, 6" (fig. 3-61) 16-22
Stegosaurus, 4.5" 16-22
Triceratops, 4.5", opalescent finish (fig. 3-62)20-25
Tyrannosaurus, 6.75", opalescent finish
    (fig. 3-63) 20-25

Fig. 3-61: Parasauralophus

Fig. 3-62: Triceratops

Fig. 3-63: Tyrannosaurus

UNITED DESIGNS (ANIMAL CLASSICS)

Triceratops, green with purple horns, painted
   resin, 10" long, 1988 (fig. 3-64) $35-50
Tyrannosaurus, green w/cream-colored belly,
   brown base, 10.5" tall, 1988 (fig. 3-65) . . 35-50

Fig. 3-64: Triceratops

Fig. 3-65: Tyrannosaurus

WADE

Wade ceramics are characterized by their diminutive size (1-2 inches), watercolor-like glaze, and grassy base. The company has developed its own collector following, and has issued a wide variety of figurines—mostly animals—including a few dinosaurs.

Ankylosaurus, brown on green base, 1"
   (fig. 3-66) $15-20
Brachiosaurus, standing on hind legs, 2" . . 15-20
Protoceratops, 1" 15-20
Spinosaurus, standing upright on brown
   base, 2" (fig. 3-67) 15-20
Tyrannosaurus, walking on green base, 2" . 15-20

Fig. 3-68: Hatching Maiasaur

Fig. 3-66: Ankylosaurus

Fig. 3-67: Spinosaurus

WINDSTONE EDITIONS

Melody Peña designed a delightful series of dinosaur hatchlings and babies for Windstone Edition, a Hollywood-based company, in the 1980s-1990s. All of the pieces in this line were discontinued in September, 1998.

Fig. 3-69: Hatching Tyrannosaurus Rex

Baby Stegosaurus, 6" long $35-45
Baby Triceratops, 7" long 35-45
Hatching Maiasaur, 6.5" long, 1989
   (fig. 3-68) 35-50
Hatching Protoceratops, 7", 1986 40-55
Hatching Tyrannosaurus Rex, 7" tall
   (fig. 3-69) 45-60
Hatching Velociraptor, 8", 1993 (fig. 3-70) . . 45-60

Fig. 3-70: Hatching Velociraptor

OTHER CERAMIC AND RESIN FIGURES

Twelve-piece painted resin set from Hong Kong, 1-2 inches tall on round base, no mark

Albertosaurus holding plant	$5-10
Allosaurus with firewood	5-10
Ankylosaurus (fig. 3-71)	5-10
Brachiosaurus	5-10
Brontosaurus	5-10
Dilophosaurus with rib cage	5-10
Eryops	5-10
Saltosaurus (orange) (fig. 3-72)	5-10
Sauropod with spikes (fig. 3-73)	5-10
Triceratops (fig. 3-74)	5-10
Tyrannosaurus with skull	5-10

Fig. 3-71: Ankylosaurus

Fig. 3-72: Saltosaurus

Fig. 3-74: Triceratops

Fig. 3-73: Sauropod with spikes

MODEL KITS

If you are a baby boomer, you might have had kit airplanes hanging from the ceiling of your room, plus kit monsters and cars on every level surface of your bookshelf. Odds are also good that at least one dinosaur model had its long neck poking out from between some books, or showing its sharp teeth next to your desk lamp. Children have always loved dinosaurs. Consequently, they have remained an ever-popular subject for plastic model kit companies.

The first company known to produce a dinosaur model kit was the Ideal Toy Company (ITC), a pioneer in the model kit industry. ITC issued a 16-inch-long, 9-inch-high Tyrannosaurus Rex skeleton, and a 12-inch-long Stegosaurus skeleton, in 1957. The kit represented the dinosaur's bones, assembled and standing on a base as seen in natural history museums. The models originally sold for $1.79, but collectors today can expect to pay upwards of $100 each for them. Since these were the first dinosaur model kits, the value could easily double in the next decade. On the heels of these kits' popularity, ITC produced a 20-inch Brontosaurus skeleton model, along with a Neanderthal Man, in 1962. The Neanderthal model kit includes figures in both human and skeletal forms. The box art shows the caveman in an action stance. The actual kit, however, portrays him standing erect (or as erect as a Neanderthal man could stand).

ITC used the company name "Ringo" to market overstock and, in 1967, the kits were re-released under that company name. According to ITC's original box side panel, a Dimetrodon, Pterodactyl, and Triceratops were intended, but they never went into production. Although I have never seen an example, a Woolly Mammoth skeleton kit by ITC may also have gone into limited distribution. Like Ringo, "Alabe" was another marketing logo used to empty remaining warehouse stock overseas when ITC was getting out of the plastic model kit market. The kits were released under this name in Europe in the mid-1970s. Today, Glencoe Models has re-issued the prehistoric animal models.

Around the time that ITC was bringing out their dinosaur skeleton kits, Palmer Hobb-e-kits of New York issued American Mastodon and Brontosaurus skeletal model kits. As with the ITC kits, these models were difficult for children to build. For instance, the Mastodon kit consists of forty-three pieces. Due to the complexity of the model's construction and the many small parts that connected to tiny surfaces, many dads spent late evenings constructing re-released in 1965 in a slightly altered box that reads, "Natural Science Ltd."

Pyro Model Company produced four dinosaur model kits in the late 1950s that set kids back 50¢ each: the Plated Dinosaur (Stegosaurus), Tyrant Lizard (Tyrannosaurus Rex), Thunder Lizard (Brontosaurus), and Horned Dinosaur (Triceratops). Instead of model kits showing the dino's fossilized bones, Pyro used their imagination and designed dinosaur models "in the flesh." Their imagination did not always create what today is believed to be the most scientifically accurate representation of dinosaurs, even when considering what was regarded to be scientific fact in the late 1950s, but kids loved 'em nevertheless. Some of the dinosaur models included landscape bases with cavemen (and in one instance, a cavewoman) to battle with, or run from, the dinos. Of course, in reality, dinosaurs were extinct for over sixty million years before mankind arrived on Earth.

In 1968, Pyro released four more dinosaur models, the Protoceratops, Ankylosaurus, Dimetrodon, and Corythosaurus. At about the same time, the original Pyro dinosaur models were re-issued, minus

CORYTHOSAURUS

the cavepeople. A model of a Neanderthal Man and Cro-Magnon Man were also released by Pyro in the late 1960s, just about the time the company was bought out. The human figures were much more animated in their poses than the ITC Neanderthal kit, and included many accessories. The Pyro kits are finally seeing some rise in value, but their price has remained in check for many years due to their continual re-issue. Kleeware issued the ex-Pyro T-Rex and Stegosaurus in England in the 1960s.

In the early 1970s, all of the Pyro casts were reissued with the new company name of Life-Like. Life-Like also produced three kits entitled The World of Tyrannosaurus, The World of Triceratops, and The

World of Stegosaurus, in 1976. The kits were titled "Dino Scenes" and included the Pyro dinosaur kit plus a new base, plants, other smaller prehistoric animals, "cave-people," and a cardboard backdrop and wall chart showing prehistory. The three models were designed to be set up side by side to form a diorama. A disclaimer on the box read, "Humans did not exist at the same time as the dinosaurs. They are in this kit to show their size compared to dinosaurs." I suspect the truth was that Life-Like knew that kids wanted people in their dinosaur models to give them some "action." In 1977, Lindberg bought all production rights to the Life-Like kits, and began reissuing them under their own company name.

Addar, a model company started by disgruntled former Aurora Plastics Corp. employees, was in business in Brooklyn, New York, from 1973 to 1976. Their "Super Scenes" series of models included a kit of "Prehistoric Dinosaurs" (as opposed to non-prehistoric dinosaurs?) in a bottle. The 1975 snap-together clear-plastic bottle included a real cork, imitation shrubbery (lichen), a colorful background, and a Tyrannosaurus attacking an unsuspecting Struthiomimus.

The year 1967 saw the Eldon model company offer 3-D scenic kits. One included dinosaurs, plants, and a base with full-color paper background.

In 1971, the one-and-only Aurora Plastics Corporation started their ever-popular line of prehistoric animal model kits entitled, "Prehistoric Scenes." Aurora figural model kits are the most desirable of all models among collectors, and the Prehistoric Scenes are no exception. Aurora had made a fortune producing monster kits in the 1960s. Since dinosaurs and monsters were synonymous with kids, dinosaurs were a logical next step for Aurora.

Seventeen kits made up the series. Fourteen came out at about the same time, and the final three appeared a few years later. Aurora's models included not only prehistoric animals and people, but realistic settings in which to place the figures: a cave, swamp, and tar pit. The models' bases were designed to interlock and form one large diorama. Children's interests were beginning to lean toward the first video games and action figures in the 1970s. Consequently, Aurora designed their model kits to snap together, thereby allowing the parts to move and eliminating the need for glue. Several of the kits included interchangeable limbs which allowed the modeler flexibility in the look of the kit. With the addition of numerous accessories, kids had a model "action figure."

One of those "action figures" was a 1/13th scale Neanderthal Man. The model included two sets of limbs in different positions, plus numerous tools, weapons, and game. The original box art portrayed the Neanderthal battling a meat-eating Allosaurus. While this made for a dramatic scene, it, of course tossed scientific accuracy to the four winds. Later, Aurora airbrushed the Allosaurus off of the box art due to numerous complaints from consumers. Was a "scientifically hip" public outraged that Aurora would inaccurately depict two creatures—ones that actually lived a hundred million years apart—in combat? No, consumers were just feeling ripped-off because the Allosaurus wasn't actually included with the Neanderthal Man as the box art suggested.

A Cro-Magnon Man and separately-sold Cro-Magnon Woman were two more kits that included two sets of arms and legs. A large model of a cave was also produced by Aurora. The original cave box art depicted the Allosaurus again, this time waiting outside the entrance. Since it was not actually included with the cave kit, it was later "evicted" from the box art. Aurora also produced a model kit of a Saber-toothed cat that included two sets of legs. A later, larger box came out when Aurora decided to revise the cat's base. The original Allosaurus box art showed the dinosaur in combat with the saber-tooth, again without regard to chronological accuracy. When a base was later added to the Allosaurus model kit, the box was enlarged and the cat was made "extinct." Was this due to angry customers wondering where their saber-tooth was in their Allosaurus model, or was it simply a case of Aurora trying to be scientifically correct? What do you think? Boxed Aurora model kits are more valuable with the original artwork, where applicable.

A kit of a bear that Aurora originally planned to be a modern day Grizzly found its home as a Prehistoric Cave Bear instead. The Giant Bird is an attractive kit, shown defending her nest against a Kuehneosaurus, in metallic blue plastic.

The Three-horned Dinosaur (Triceratops) and Spiked Dinosaur (Styracosaurus) were large models. Although these dinosaurs were peaceful, plant-munchers in the Cretaceous Age, Aurora portrays them with evil sneers and razor sharp teeth—features likely linked to Aurora's decade of making monster models and their latest attempt to get children to buy the dinosaurs.

Many of Aurora's model kits have been reissued by Monogram, which bought the company in 1977. Some of the molds have been lost, however, making those kits more valuable today. The Jungle Swamp model kit was an interesting addition to the Prehistoric Scenes line. It consisted of over thirty parts, including a pond base, several trees, and various prehistoric animals in two different colors of plastic. It is certain that this mold has been lost, making this kit now worth over $100 to collectors.

In 1974, the Armored Dinosaur (Ankylosaurus) was released, and in 1975, the Sailback Reptile (Dimetrodon) and the huge Tyrannosaurus Rex kit finished up the line. The T-Rex stood 18 inches tall and was almost a yard long. It cost a whopping $15 when it first came out, and sells for over $200 to collectors today. The Ankylosaurus saw limited distribution. The Sailback was cast in copper-colored plastic with see-through green colored plants. The T-Rex was cast in red plastic with glow-in-the-dark eyes, claws, and teeth. All of the Prehistoric Scenes kits sold well for Aurora and were finely detailed and crafted. The Aurora Prehistoric Scenes models are every dinosaur modeler's favorites.

I once interviewed renowned comic book artist Dave Cockrum, who also doubled as a model designer for Aurora in the 1970s. It was Dave who designed Aurora's Tyrannosaurus Rex model (although the top brass at Aurora added the extra large teeth to the kit). He told me of many dinosaurs that Aurora considered adding to the line just before they called it quits (Parasaurolophus, Deinonychus, Archaeopteryx, a huge King Kong to battle the T-Rex, etc.). Dave's design of a large Stegosaurus was completely sculpted in clay, but never went into production. A few years ago, Lunar Models re-sculpted the "Aurora Stegosaurus," using photographs of the master, and produced it in resin.

Collectible dinosaur models aren't only produced in the United States. The British company known as Airfix came out with some fine dinosaur kits in the late 1970s and early 1980s. MPC later reissued some of these dinosaur kits. Bandai, of Japan, made a series of eight dinosaur models in various "scales" (no pun intended) in the 1970s. The eight kits included a mechanical motor, and were designed to be wound-up for movement. The box art on these kits was superb. Eidai and Nitto, of Japan, produced four small plastic dinosaur assembly kits before going out of business. In 1982, the Japanese firm, Tamiya, changed direction from their usual military and automobile kits to produce three dinosaur models. A later Pteranodon, packaged in a bag, was also issued but saw little distribution in America. It was originally designed as a give-away for visitors to the Tamiya manufacturing plant. In the early 1990s, Tamiya produced a new series of very realistic and scientifically accurate dinosaur models that made many dino fans happy. The box art was, arguably, the best ever seen.

Talented adult artists and collectors hungry for model kits of various subject matters, including dinosaurs, began to sculpt their own models in the 1980s. They filled rubber molds with a plastic resin material, thereby creating some of the most beautifully sculpted models ever. The "garage kit" (so called because many kits were made in garages) became a cottage industry that continues to grow to this day. Although it began in Japan, it continues to evolve internationally as a cottage industry, especially in the United States. Japanese companies like Tsukuda and Kaiyodo produced resin and vinyl model kits of dinosaurs in Japan, and it wasn't long before pioneering American companies such as Phil Bracco's Distinct Extinctions, Mike Evans' Lunar Models, and Scott Kelley's Alternative Images were also producing dinosaur resin kits. The business continues to branch out, involving many gifted sculptors and creating most every dinosaur known to science—with no end in sight.

—*Mike Fredericks*

DINOSAUR MODEL KITS
Value Guide

All prices are for un-built kits, mint in package. On classic store-bought plastic kits, build-ups generally bring half the value. However, on the newer high-end resin and vinyl kits, prices for models already built and painted may be three or four times the original un-built price. This is because, typically, plastic models have been built and painted by a youngster, while new resin kits, often available built and painted from the studio, have been skillfully detailed by an accomplished artist.

Fig. 4-1: Airfix model kit for a Corythosaurus

ACTION HOBBIES
Resin model kits, 1990s

Mosasaur scene, by Cockrum $60-80
Velociraptor, starting to run 30-50

ADDAR
Plastic model kits, 1970s

Prehistoric Dinosaurs, Super Scenes
   series, 1976 . . . . $40-50

AIRFIX
Plastic model kits, from
Britain/France, 1960s-1980s

Ankylosaurus, 1978 . . . . $25-35
Brontosaurus, 1982 25-35
Corythosaurus, 1979 (fig. 4-1) 30-40
Dimetrodon, 1979 25-35

Pteranodon, 1980 . . . . $35-50
Stegosaurus, 1978 (figs. 4-2 and 4-3) . . . 25-35
Triceratops, 1976 (fig. 4-4) 25-35
Tyrannosaurus Rex, 14", 1976
   (figs. 4-5 and 4-6) 25-35

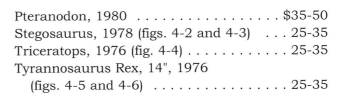
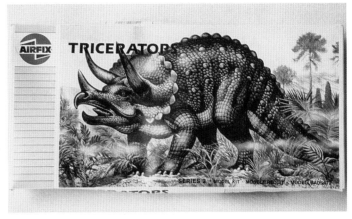

Fig. 4-4: Triceratops kit, from Airfix

Fig. 4-2: Airfix kit for a Stegosaurus

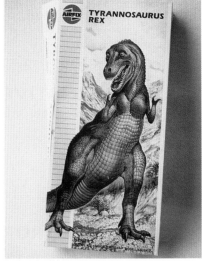

Fig. 4-5: Tyrannosaurus Rex
kit, by Airfix

Fig. 4-3: Completed Airfix Stegosaurus

Fig. 4-6: Tyrannosaurus Rex, by Airfix, in
completed form

U.S. AIRFIX
1980, and Airfix/Humbrol, 1989

Dimetrodon $8-12
Stegosaurus 8-12
Triceratops, ... 8-12
Tyrannosaurus, 14" long 8-12

ALCHEMY WORKS
Resin kits by Mike Evans, 1990s

Amargasaurus $150-200
Arsinitherium vs. Dire Wolf 140-170
Estemmosuchus 100-125
Postosuchus vs. Desmatosuchus 150-200
Stegosaurus, 21" 175-225
Yangchuanosaurus Shangyouensis,
  by Thomas Dickens 160-190
Zallinger Permian Diorama 75-125
Zallinger Plateosaurus
  (Age of Reptiles mural) 50-75
Zallinger Pteranodon
  (Age of Reptiles mural) 30-50
Zallinger Trachodon
  (Age of Reptiles mural) 50-75

ALTERNATIVE IMAGES
Resin model kits, 1990s

Allosaurus $120-250
Velociraptor (The Raptor), 1993
  (fig. 4-7) 100-125

AURORA
Prehistoric Scenes, plastic kits, 1971

Allosaurus, #736, 1/13 scale, green
  and yellow plastic $90-125
Armored Dinosaur (Ankylosaurus),
  #744, 1/13 scale, orange plastic 90-125
Cave (The), #732, 1/13 scale,
  gray plastic 40-50
Cave Bear, #738, 1/13 scale, dark brown
  plastic (fig. 4-8) 40-50
Cro-Magnon Man, #730, 1/13 scale,
  tan plastic 20-30
Cro-Magnon Woman, #731, 1/13 scale,
  tan plastic (fig. 4-9) 30-40
Flying Reptile, #734, 1/13 scale, orange
  plastic (figs. 4-10 and 4-11) 50-75
Giant Bird, #739, 1/13 scale, blue-silver
  plastic 40-50

Fig. 4-7: Alternative Images' Velociraptor (The Raptor) kit

Fig. 4-8: Aurora kit: Cave Bear

Fig. 4-10: Aurora's Flying Reptile kit

Fig. 4-9: Aurora kit: Cro-Magnon Woman

Fig. 4-11: Flying Reptile, built-up

Fig. 4-12: Aurora's Saber-Toothed Tiger

Fig. 4-13: Saber-Toothed Tiger, built-up

Fig. 4-14: Spiked Dinosaur, by Aurora

Fig. 4-15: Three-Horned Dinosaur kit, by Aurora

Jungle Swamp, #740, 1/13 scale, orange
    and green plastic $50-75
Neanderthal Man, #729, 1/13 scale,
    tan plastic 20-30
Saber-Toothed Tiger, #733, 1/13 scale,
    yellow plastic (figs. 4-12 and 4-13) 30-40
Sail Back Reptile (Dimetrodon), #745,
    1/13 scale, copper, green plastic 50-75
Spiked Dinosaur, #742, 1/13 scale, tan
    and green plastic (fig. 4-14) 70-85
Tar Pit, #735, 1/13 scale, orange plastic . 40-50
Three-Horned Dinosaur (Triceratops),
    #741, 1/13 scale, silver plastic
    (figs. 4-15 and 4-16) 70-85
Tyrannosaurus Rex, #746, 1/13 scale
    (35" long), red plastic with glow parts
    (fig. 4-17) 150-200
Woolly Mammoth, #743, 1/13 scale
    (18" long), green and cream plastic . . . 90-125

Fig. 4-16: Three-Horned Dinosaur, built-up

Fig. 4-17: Box art for Aurora
Tyrannosaurus Rex kit

Fig. 4-18: T-Rex, from a Charles McGrady resin kit

Fig. 4-19: Baryonyx—Cretaceous Creations kit

Fig. 4-20: Iguanodon—Cretaceous Creations kit

Fig. 4-21: Baby Allosaurus skull, by Dana Gerath

BANDAI
Wind-up plastic model kits, Japanese, 1970s

Ankylosaurus, 1/17 . . . . $40-60
Brontosaurus, 1/35 40-60
Dimetrodon, 1/14 40-60
Iguanodon, 1/35 40-60
Stegosaurus, 1/35 40-60
Styracosaurus, 1/20 40-60
Triceratops, 1/26 40-60
Tyrannosaurus, 1/35 40-60

BOWMAN ARTS STUDIO
Resin kits by Bruce Bowman, 1990s

Velociraptor (feathered), 1/5 . . . . $90-110

CM STUDIO
Resin kits by Charles McGrady, 1990s

Albertosaurus, 1/20, 18" $100-150
Styracosaurus, 1/20, 11" 75-100
T-Rex, 1/18, 32" (fig. 4-18) 200-250
Utahraptor, 1/8 200-250
Stegosaurus, 1/12 175-225
T-Rex, 1/12, 45" 450-550

CONTINENTAL CREATURES
Resin kits by Cliff Green, 1990s

Acrocanthosaurus with Tenontosaurus
    prey $100-150
Carcharodontosaurus Saharilous, 1/24 . 80-120
Elasmotherium 80-120
Giganotosaurus Carolinii, 1/24 100-130
Shonosaurus with base 120-160
Torosaurus Latus, 1/24 75-100

CRETACEOUS CREATIONS
Resin kits by Shane Foulkes, 1990s

Baryonyx , 1/18, 19" (fig. 4-19) $80-110
Iguanodon, 1/18, 17" (fig. 4-20) 80-110
Pentaceratops, 1/18 80-110

DAN LORUSSO
Resin kits, 1990s
Mosasaur, 1/35 . . . . $80-100

DANA GERATH STUDIO
Resin model kits, 1990s

Baby Allosaurus skull (fig. 4-21) $100-140
Dilophosaurus Wetherilli, 1/10 150-175

Elasmosaurus and calf $150-175
Ioraptor bust (fig. 4-22) 175-225
Liopleurodon, 1/20 150-175
Oviraptor on nest (fig. 4-23) 150-175
Velociraptor skull 160-180

DAVID KRENTZ
Resin kits, 1990s

Einiosaurus, "Buffalo Bull," 14", 1998 .$100-120
Gorgosaurus, 1/18, 20", 1998
   (fig. 4-24) 120-150

DINO STUDIO
One-piece, unpainted resin kits
by LoRusso & Wenzel, 1990s

Albertosaurus, 1/35 . . . . $75-100
Allosaurus, 1/35 75-100
Cryolophosaurus skull, 1/3 350-400
Lambeosaurus, 1/35 75-100
Stegosaurus, 1/35 75-100
Triceratops, 1/35 75-100

DISTINCT EXTINCTIONS
Resin kits by Phil Bracco, early 1990s

Kit #1, Nanotyrannus with prey,
   10" x 8", out of print $150-200
Kit #2, Avimimus, 9.5" x 8",
   out of print 120-180
Kit #3, Dunkleosteos, 8" long,
   out of print 100-150
Kit #4, Amargasaurus, 7" x 5",
   out of print 75-100
Kit #5, Savage Eden (fighting theropods),
   10" x 8", out of print 200-250

DRAGON ATTACK
Resin kits, 1990s

Brachiosaurus, 1/35 . . . . $200-250
Metriacanthosaurus, 1/20 130-160

DRAGON INC
Resin kits by Keith Strasser, 1990s

Dimetrodon, 21", 1/5 (fig. 4-25) $100-150
Diplodocus, 1/20 500-650
Edaphosaurus Posonias, 20", 1/5 100-150
Lambeosaurus, 1/20, Triceratops Hills
   Ranch exclusive 225-275
Ouranosaurus, 1/20 100-135
Pachycephalosaurus, 1/20 75-125

Fig. 4-22: Ioraptor bust, by Dana Gerath

Fig. 4-23: Dana Gerath's Oviraptor on nest

Fig. 4-24: Gorgosaurus, by David Krentz

Fig. 4-25: Dimetrodon, by Keith Strasser

Fig. 4-26: 3-D Scenic Dinosaurs, by Eldon

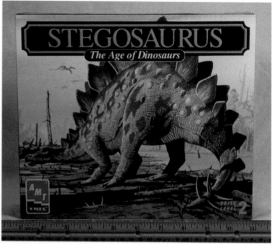

Fig. 4-27: Stegosaurus kit, by Ertl/AMT

Fig. 4-28: Brontosaurus skeleton kit, from Glencoe

Fig. 4-29: Stegosaurus skeleton kit, from Glencoe

Spinosaurus, 1/20 . . . . $175-225
Triceratops, 1/20 125-175
Tyrannosaurus, 1/20 400-500
Suchomimus, 1/20 125-175
Wall-mounted head, Carnotaurus 75-125
Wall-mounted head, Ceratosaurus 75-125
Wall-mounted head, Dilophosaurus 75-125
Wall-mounted head, T-Rex 75-125
Wall-mounted head, T-Rex skull 75-125
Wall-mounted head, Utahraptor 75-125

DREAMSTAR
Resin kits by John Fischner, 1990s

Apatosaurus hatchling, 5" $30-40
Camarasaurus hatchling, 7" 30-40
Ceratosaurus hatchling 30-40
Edmontosaurus hatchling, 5.5" 30-40
Stegosaurus hatchling, 5" 30-40
Struthomimus hatchling 30-40
Triceratops hatchling, 4" 30-40
Tyrannosaurus hatchling, 5.5" 30-40
Velociraptor hatchling, deluxe kit, 1/15 . . 30-40

EIDAI
Plastic Japanese kits, 1975

Brontosaurus, 4", 1975 . . . . $20-30
Pteranodon, 4", 1975 20-30
Stegosaurus, 4", 1975 20-30
Tyrannosaurus, 4", 1975 20-30

ELDON
Plastic model kits, 1960s

3-D Scenic Dinosaurs, 1967 (fig. 4-26) . . $60-80

ERTL/AMT
(Airfix re-issues), plastic kits, mid-1990s

Stegosaurus (fig. 4-27) $7-10
Triceratops 7-10
Tyrannosaurus 7-10

GLENCOE
Plastic model kits (ITC re-issues), 1990s

Brontosaurus skeleton, 1995 (fig. 4-28) . . $8-12
Stegosaurus skeleton (fig. 4-29) 8-12
T-Rex skeleton 8-12

Fig. 4-30: Horizon's Hunting Velociraptor

Fig. 4-31: Close-up detail of Horizon's Velociraptor

HORIZON
Resin model kits, 1980s-1990s

Apatosaurus, 1/30 . . . . $35-45
Archaeopteryx Lithographica, Fossil
    Reproduction Collection, 9" 35-45
Archaeopteryx with feathers, Fossil
    Reproduction Collection. 35-45
Elasmosaurus, 1/30 35-45
Coelophysis, Fossil Reproduction
    Collection, 18" 40-55
Hunting Velociraptor (Darga), 30" long
    (figs. 4-30 and 4-31) 65-75
Life-size Hatchling T-Rex (Darga) 55-70
Pteradactylus Kochi, adult, Fossil
    Reproduction Collection, 7" x 9" 35-45
Pteradactylus Kochi, juvenile, Fossil
    Reproduction Collection, 7.5" x 7" 25-35
Rhamphorhynchus, Fossil Reproduction
    Collection, 11" x 5" 35-45
Stegosaurus, 1/30 (fig. 4-32) 35-45
Tyrannosaurus Rex, 1/30 (fig. 4-33) 40-60

ITC, IDEAL TOY COMPANY
Plastic kits, 1957-1962

Brontosaurus skeleton 1/35, 20",
    1962 . . . . $75-125
Mammoth skeleton,
    rumored to exist . . . . .no known sales
Neanderthal Man, 1/8, 1962 60-90
Stegosaurus skeleton, 1/25, 12", 1957 . . 75-125
Tyrannosaurus Rex skeleton, 1/25, 16",
    1957 75-125

Fig. 4-32: Stegosaurus kit, from Horizon

Fig. 4-33: Horizon's Tyrannosaurus Rex, as painted by Jerry Finney

Fig. 4-34: Kaiyodo Dinoland Series model kit

Fig. 4-35: Kaiyodo's Camarasaurus, built-up

JERRY FINNEY
Resin kits, 1990s

Acrocanthosaurus with base, 1/35 . . . $100-120
Smilodon, 1/20 20-35
Smilodon with Clovis Hunter, 1/20 60-80
Tnojiaugosaurus (Asian Stegosaurus),
    1/35 80-120
Woolly Rhino, with base, 1/35 40-60

KAIYODO
Japanese resin and vinyl model kits, 1980s-1990s

"Dinosaur Collection," 1/35 scale resin kits, bagged with header card, 1987

Brachiosaurus $20-35
Brontosaurus 20-35
Camptosaurus 20-35
Dimetrodon 20-35
Dimorphodon 20-35
Hypacrosaurus 20-35
Ichthyosaurus 20-35
Kentrosaurus 20-35
Megalosaurus 20-35
Melanorosaurus 20-35
Monoclonius 20-35
Parasaurolophus 20-35
Scolosaurus 20-35
Tarbosaurus 20-35
Triceratops 20-35
Tuojiangosaurus 20-35
Tyrannosaurus 20-35

1/20 scale vinyl model kits

Anchiceratops $55-65
Ankylosaurus 55-65
Brachiosaurus 150-175
Chasmosaurus 45-55
Parasaurolophys 50-60
Saltasaurus 60-70
Stegosaurus 60-70
Styracosaurus 50-60
Triceratops 50-60

Dinoland series, 1/35 scale vinyl model kits (fig. 4-34)

Camarasaurus (fig. 4-35) $25-35
Maiasura 25-35
Triceratops 25-35

Resin model kits

Allosaurus, Dinoland series, 1/100 . . . . $12-20
Amargasaurus 150-200
Archelon prehistoric turtle 175-225
Barosaurus and baby vs. Allosaurus,
    1/35 350-425
Ceratosaurus, 1/20, 17" long 175-225
Chasmosaurus, 1/35, with base 75-125
Deinonychus, 1/10 120-160
Dilophosaurus 45-55
Euoplocephalus, 1/35 75-125
Hemicyclaspis, armored fish, life size 70-90
Megalosaur eating Polocanthus 125-175
Nautaloid and Trilobites, 1/5 140-175
Pachycephalosaurus pair, 1/35 175-200
Plesiosaur, 1/35 120-150
Prehistoric Meiolania turtle 200-225

Fig. 4-36: Kaiyodo's Velociraptor and Protoceratops

Fig. 4-37: Tyrant King Tyrannosaurus kit, from Life-Like

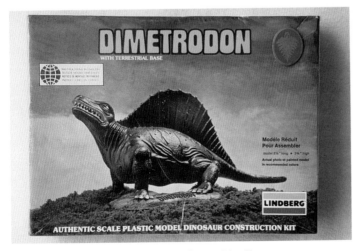

Fig. 4-38: Dimetrodon kit, from Lindberg

Saichania, 1/35 . . . . $110-140
Tylosaurus, 1/35 120-160
Tyrannosaurus, roaring, 1/35 130-170
Velociraptor 120-150
Velociraptor and Protoceratops, 1/10
   (fig. 4-36) 160-180
Velociraptor skull, life size 175-225

KLEEWARE
British Pyro re-issue kits, late 1950s

Stegosaurus skeleton, 1/25, 12" $70-100
Tyrannosaurus, 1/48 20-40

LIFE-LIKE HOBBY KITS
Plastic kits (re-issued Pyro), 1970s

Ankylosaurus (Fortress Lizard),
   1/32, 1973 . . . .$20-40
Corythosaurus, 1/35, 1973 20-40
Cro-Magnon Man, 1/8, 1973 30-50
Dimetrodon, 1/10, 1973 20-40
Horned Dinosaur Triceratops, 1/40, 1973 20-40
Neanderthal Man, 1/8, 1973 30-50
Plated Lizard Stegosaurus, 1/32, 1973 . . .20-40
Protoceratops, 1/8 20-40
Thunder Lizard Brontosaurus, 1/72,
   1973 20-40
Tyrant King Tyrannosaurus, 1/48,
   purple plastic (fig. 4-37) 20-40

Life-like "World of . . ." plastic model kits

Stegosaurus, 1/32, 1977 . . . .$30-50
Triceratops, 1/40, 1977 30-50
Tyrannosaurus, 1/48, 1977 30-50

LINDBERG
Plastic model kits (Pyro re-issues), 1979

Brontosaurus $10-18
Dimetrodon, 8.25" long (fig. 4-38) 10-18
Stegosaurus 10-18
Tyrannosaurus 10-18

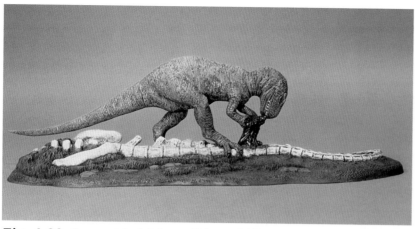

Fig. 4-39: Lunar Models' rendition of Allosaurus eating Brontosaurus

Fig. 4-42: Lunar Models' Kronosaurus

Fig. 4-40: Lunar Models' Barosaurus family (unpainted)

Fig. 4-41: Lunar Models' Barosaurus family (painted)

Fig. 4-43: Lunar's Protoceratops vs. Velociraptor, by Bob Morales

LUNAR MODELS
Resin kits, 1980s-1990s

Sculptor's name in parentheses

Albertosaurus $80-110
Allosaurus, Zallinger series 55-75
Allosaurus eating Brontosaurus (Knight)
    (fig. 4-39) 100-120
Ankylosaurus, Zallinger series 55-75
Arsinotherium 160-190
Barosaurus family (Morales)
    (figs. 4-40 and 4-41) 140-170
Brontosaurus, Zallinger series 80-100
Burian diorama with six dinosaurs,
    16" base 120-150
Carnotaurus, large limited edition
    (Morales) 175-225
Carnotaurus vs. Hypacrosaurus
    (Morales) 120-140
Ceratosaurus vs. Stegosaurus
    (Morales) 120-150

Dimetrodon and Diplocaulus (Morales) . $90-120
Elasmosaurus (Evans), 1/48, 1986 30-45
Elasmotherium 80-110
Kronosaurus (Johnson) (fig. 4-42) 100-140
Mamenchisaurus, limited edition
    (Morales) 175-225
Pachyrhinosaurus (Morales) 120-160
Platybelodon (Morales) 150-190
Protoceratops vs. Velociraptor (Morales)
    (fig. 4-43) 100-140
Quetzalcoatlus vs. Albertosaurus
    (Morales) 150-200
Stegosaurus, Zallinger series 55-75
Triceratops, Zallinger series 55-75
T-Rex vs. Edmontonia (Morales)
    (fig. 4-44) 100-135
T-Rex vs. Raptors (Morales) (fig. 4-45) . 120-150
Tyrannosaurus, 1/48, 8" (Evans), 1987 . . 30-40
Tyrannosaurus, 31" long 250-320
Tyrannosaurus Mural, Zallinger series . . . 50-75
Unitatherium and baby (fig. 4-46) 100-120

Fig. 4-44: Lunar's T-Rex vs. Edmontonia, by Bob Morales

Fig. 4-45: Lunar's T-Rex vs. Raptors, by Bob Morales

Fig. 4-46: Lunar's Unitatherium and baby

Fig. 4-47: Deinonychus resin model, by Matt Manit

Fig. 4-48: Stegosaurus, from Michael Furuya Studio

MATT MANIT
Resin kits, 1990s

Deinonychus, 1/8 (fig. 4-47) $80-100
Protoceratops, 1/8 80-100

MAXIMO SALAS
Resin kits, 1989-1990

Argentinosaurus, 38" $200-250
Omeiosaurus, 1/35 90-120
Saltosaurus, 1/35 75-100
Seismosaurus, 1/35 175-200

MENAGERIE PRODUCTIONS
Resin kits by Tony McVey, 1990s

Striding T-Rex, 1/30 . . . . $150-200

MICHAEL FURUYA STUDIO
Resin kits, 1990s

Stegosaurus, 1/20 (fig. 4-48) $150-175
Tyrannosaurus, 1/20 200-250

MONOGRAM
Plastic model kits (re-issued Aurora), 1979-1980

Allosaurus, 1/13, 1979 and 1987 ..... $25-35
Ankylosaurus, 1/13, 1979 and 1987 20-30
Dimetrodon, 1/13, 1979 and 1987 15-25
Pteranodon, 1987 (fig. 4-49) 30-40
Styracosaurus, 1987 (fig. 4-50) 30-40
Triceratops, 1987 (fig. 4-51) 30-40
Tyrannosaurus rex, 1/13, 1979 and 1987   40-55
Woolly Mammoth, Giant, 1/13, 1979 and 1987
   (fig. 4-52) 30-40

Fig. 4-53: Stegosaurus kit, from MPC

Fig. 4-49: Monogram kit—Pteranodon

Fig. 4-50: Monogram
kit—Styracosaurus

Fig. 4-51: Monogram
kit—Triceratops

Fig. 4-52: Monogram kit—Giant Woolly
Mammoth

MPC
Plastic model kits (re-issued Airfix), 1982

Brontosaurus $10-20
Stegosaurus (fig. 4-53) 10-20
Triceratops 10-20
Tyrannosaurus, 14" 10-20

NATURAL SCIENCE (NSI)
Plastic kits (re-issued Palmer), mid-1960s

American Mastodon skeleton $20-30
Brontosaurus skeleton 20-30

NITTO
Japanese plastic kits, mid-1980s

Brontosaurus, 4" $20-30
Stegosaurus, 4" 20-30
Triceratops, 4" 20-30
Tyrannosaurus, 4" 20-30

PALEOCRAFT
Resin kits by Sean Cooper, 1990s

Indricotherium $50-75
Woolly Rhino with baby 50-75

PALMER
Plastic model kits, late 1950s

American Mastodon skeleton, 10"
   (fig. 4-54, top) $20-40
Brontosaurus skeleton 13"
   (fig. 4-54, bottom) 20-40

Fig. 4-54 (top): Palmer's American Mastodon kit
Fig. 4-54 (bottom): Palmer's Brontosaurus kit

Fig. 4-55: Ankylosaurus plastic model, from Pyro

PYRO
Plastic model kits, late 1950s-late 1960s

Ankylosaurus, 1/32 (fig. 4-55) $20-40
Corythosaurus, 1/35 (figs. 4-56 and 4-57) 20-40
Cro-Magnon Man, 1/8 30-50
Dimetrodon, 1/10 (figs. 4-58 and 4-59) . . 20-40
Horned Dinosaur, Triceratops, 1/40 20-40
Neanderthal Man, 1/8, 1968 30-50

Fig. 4-56: Corythosaurus kit, by Pyro

Fig. 4-57: Corythosaurus, completed Pyro model

Fig. 4-58: Dimetrodon kit, by Pyro

Fig. 4-59: Dimetrodon, completed Pyro model

Fig. 4-60: Original packaging for Pyro's Plated Dinosaur (Stegosaurus), circa 1950s

Fig. 4-61: Later Pyro model packaging for Plated Dinosaur (Stegosaurus)

Fig. 4-62: Built-up model of Pyro's Stegosaurus

Fig. 4-63: Ankylosaurus kit, from Revell

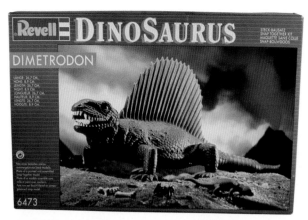

Fig. 4-64: Dimetrodon kit, from Revell

Fig. 4-65: Pteranodon kit, from Revell   **Fig. 4-66:** Triceratops kit, from Revell

Plated Dinosaur, Stegosaurus, 1/32
    (figs. 4-60, 4-61, and 4-62) $20-40
Protoceratops, 1/8 20-40
Thunder Lizard, Brontosaurus, 1/72, 11" . 20-40
Tyrant King, Tyrannosaurus, 1/48, 10" . . 20-40

REAL DINO
One-piece bisque model kits with paints, 1990s

Brachiosaurus $15-20
Stegosaurus 15-20
Triceratops 15-20
Tyrannosaurus 15-20

REVELL/MONOGRAM
Plastic kits (re-issued Aurora), 1990s

Allosaurus, 1/13, 1992 . . . . $15-25
Ankylosaurus, 1/13, 1993 (fig. 4-63) 20-30
Dimetrodon, 1/13, 1992 (fig. 4-64) 12-20
Pteranodon, 1/13, 1992 (fig. 4-65) 15-25
Triceratops, 1993 (fig. 4-66) 20-30

Revell Quick Snap Dinos
(tiny 1/100 versions of Aurora kits), 1994

Allosaurus $4-8
Dimetrodon 4-8
Pteranodon 4-8

Styracosaurus $4-8
Triceratops 4-8
Tyrannosaurus Rex 4-8

RINGO
Plastic kits (re-issue of ITC), 1967

Brontosaurus skeleton, 1/35, 20" $60-80
Neanderthal Man, 1/8 60-80
Stegosaurus skeleton, 1/25, 12" 60-80
Tyrannosaurus Rex skeleton, 1/25, 16" . . 60-80

SAURIAN STUDIOS
Resin kits, 1990s

Sculptor's name in parentheses
Acrocanthosaurus, 1/20
   (without base) $175-225
Alioramus (Jones), 1/12, 18" with base . 100-140
Alioramus, 48" long 450-550
Anchiceratops (Mike Jones), 1/10, 26" . 500-600
Archaeopteryx, life size (Jerry Finney) . . 175-225
Arrhinoceratops (Mike Jones),
   1/10, 26" 450-550
Astrodon, sauropod in defensive
   posture (Jerry Finney), 1/35 125-165
Astrodon (as above) with four
   Utahraptors, diorama (Jerry Finney),
   1/35, without base (fig. 4-67) 240-280
Avaceratops (Jones), 1/10 120-150
Brachyceratops (Jones), 1/10 120-150
Carcharodontosaurus, 1/20 200-250
Carnotaurus (Max Salas), 1/20 100-125
Carnotaurus and prey (McVey) 140-180
Centrosaurus bust (Mike Jones), 10" . . 145-175
Ceratosaurus (Jerry Finney), 1/10 160-190
Ceratosaurus bust (Joe DeVito),
   1/6, 9" 120-160
Ceratosaurus juveniles, pair
   (Jerry Finney), 1/10 40-60
Chasmosaurus bust, female
   (Mike Jones), 9" 130-170
Chasmosaurus bust, male
   (Mike Jones), 10" 130-170
Compsognathus, life size (Jerry Finney) .150-200
Cryolophosaurus pair with prey
   (Max Salas), 1/20 225-275
Cynognathus and prey (Max Salas),
   1/10 140-170
Deinonychus (Alderson), 1/5, 26" 175-200
Epantarias (large Allosaurus), 1/20 . . . 150-200
Gigantosaurus (Max Salas), 1/20 200-250
Glyptodont (Max Salas), 1/10 100-125
La Brea Diorama (Mastodon,
   2 Smilodons, 2 Vultures), 1/10 550-650

Fig. 4-67: Astrodon with four Utahraptors, in a diorama by Jerry Finney

Fig. 4-68: Saurian Studios' completed model of Tyrannosaurus

Leptoceratops (Jones), 1/10 . . . . $25-35
Megalodon shark (Jerry Finney), 1/35 . . 80-120
Megalosaurus (Max Salas), 1/20 80-120
Microceratops (Jones), 1/10 25-35
Microceratops, life size, 30" (Mike Jones) 550-650
Monolophosaurus (Mike Jones),
   1/24, 12" 75-100
Montanoceratops (Jones), 1/10 70-100
Nanotyrannus (Jerry Finney), 1/5 350-450
Nanotyrannus and Struthiomimus,
   1/10 140-180
Phororachus (M. Salas) 80-120
Pteranodon (Penkalski), 1/15, 20" 100-135
Protoceratops, style A (Mike Jones) 125-165
Protoceratops, style B (Mike Jones) . . . 110-140
Spinosaurus, 1/20 160-200
Struthiomimus (Jerry Finney), 1/10 . . . 125-175
Struthiomimus (Jerry Finney), 1/5 250-350
Stygimoloch (Jones), 1/5, 23" long 150-200
Therizinosaurus, 48" long 450-550
Thylacosmilus (Max Salas), 1/10 80-120
Titanosuchus (Mike Jones), 1/10 35-50
Triceratops bust (Mike Jones), 24" 450-550
Tyrannosaurus, 1/20 (fig. 4-68) 175-225
Tyrannosaurus hatchling (Bill Weiger) . . . 50-75

Fig. 4-69: Tamiya Brachiosaurus diorama

Fig. 4-70: Tamiya's Chasmosaurus with baby, diorama kit

Fig. 4-71: Tamiya's Chasmosaurus with baby, completed diorama

Tyrannosaurus juveniles diorama,
  life size, five animals $300-350
Utahraptor #1, mouth open, head turned
  (Jerry Finney), 1/35 30-40
Utahraptor #2, mouth closed
  (Jerry Finney), 1/35 30-40
Utahraptor #3, injured (J. Finney), 1/35 . . . 30-40
Utahraptor #4, attacking
  (Jerry Finney), 1/35 30-40

SHAWN NAGLE
Resin kits, 1990s

"Charge," Styracosaurus, based on
  William Stout art, 1998 . . . . $75-100

SKILCRAFT
Plastic model kits, 1990s

Allosaurus vs. Pteranodon (both from
  Aurora molds), 1/13 scale, 1993 . . . . $40-55

TAMIYA
Plastic model kits, Japanese, 1980s-1990s

Brachiosaurus diorama, 1994
  (fig. 4-69) $70-90
Chasmosaurus with baby, diorama,
  1994 (figs. 4-70 and 4-71) 25-35
Mesozoic Creatures (6 different), 1994
  (fig. 4-72) 15-25
Parasaurolophus and Nyctosaur
  diorama, 1994 (figs. 4-73 and 4-74) . . . 25-35
Pteranodon, 1/35, 1986 20-30
Stegosaurus, 1/35, 4.5", 1982 10-15
Triceratops, 1/35, 3", 1982 10-15
Triceratops with Velociraptor diorama,
  1994 (figs. 4-75 and 4-76) 35-45
Tyrannosaurus Rex, 1/35, 10", 1982 10-15
Tyrannosaurus Rex with figure diorama,
  1994 40-50
Velociraptor pack (6 different), 1.5-2",
  1994 (figs. 4-77 and 4-78) 15-25

Fig. 4-72: Mesozoic Creatures

Fig. 4-73: Tamiya's Parasaurolophus and Nyctosaur diorama kit

Fig. 4-74: Tamiya's Parasaurolophus and Nyctosaur diorama, built-up

Fig. 4-75: Tamiya's Triceratops with Velociraptor diorama kit

Fig. 4-76: Tamiya's Triceratops with Velociraptor diorama, built-up

Fig. 4-78: Velociraptor six-pack, built-up

WICCART
Resin kits by Steve Harvey, 1990s

Dunkleosteus $75-100
Herrerasaurus skull 150-200
Oviraptor skull 80-100
Platecarpus skull 80-100
Rhamphorhynchus skull 60-80
Riojasuchus skull 50-75
Styracosaurus skull 80-100

Fig. 4-77: Velociraptor six-pack, from Tamiya

TRCIC STUDIO
Resin kits by Michael Trcic, 1990s

Dromaeosaurus (Raptor), 1/8 . . . . $100-125
Styracosaurus bust, 1/8 100-125
T-Rex, 1/35 100-125

Fig. 5-3: Remco's Dino Hunter playset

Fig. 5-1: Dinoball

Fig. 5-2: Dinosaur coloring book, by Whitman

MORE DINOSAUR TOYS & GAMES

Fig. 5-4: Hasbro's G.I. Joe Dino-Hunter Mission playset

Fig. 5-6: National Geographic Transforming Action Set

Fig. 5-5: Hot Wheels Speed-A-Saurus, by Mattel

Fig. 5-7: Pez dinosaur head dispensers

Fig. 5-9: Plush Apatosaurus, by Applause/Determined Products

Fig. 5-8: PianoSaurus

Fig. 5-10: Plush Stegosaurus, by Animal Fair

Fig. 5-11: Plush Stegosaurus, by Dakin

Fig. 5-12: Jurassic Pets series Pogs

Plush toy, Bix from Dinotopia, Protoceratops, Wards exclusive, 1990s . $20-25

Plush toy, green Apatosaurus type dino, 5.5", Applause/Determined Products, 1992 (fig. 5-9) 3-5

Plush toy, Stegosaurus, brown and furry, 26" long, Animal Fair, no year marked (fig. 5-10) 5-10

Plush toy, Stegosaurus, gray and furry, 10.5" long, Dakin, 1980 (fig. 5-11) 4-8

Pogs, Jurassic Pets series (fig. 5-12) each 25¢-50¢

Puzzle, boxed jigsaw puzzle, National Geographic "Dinosaurs" cover, 1000 pieces (fig. 5-13) 8-12

Puzzle, wooden frame tray puzzle, various dinosaur species, Simplex, late 1960s 15-25

Ramp Walker, Ankylosaurus with clown on back, plastic, Marx, 1950s (fig. 5-14, left) 50-100

Fig. 5-14 (left): Marx Ankylosaurus Ramp Walker **(right):** Marx Brontosaurus Ramp Walker

Fig. 5-13: National Geographic Dinosaurs puzzle

Fig. 5-15: Kenner's build-a-skeleton Tyrannosaurus

Fig. 5-16: Built-up Kenner Tyrannosaurus with Mike Fredericks' kids.

Ramp Walker, Brontosaurus with monkey
   on back, plastic, Marx, 1950s
   (fig. 5-14, right) $50-100
Rex, the Tyrannosaurus—build-a-skeleton
   from 30 Styrofoam bones, 6' long,
   Kenner, 1960s (figs. 5-15 and 5-16) . . 150-200
Strange Change Toy: The Lost World,
   15" x 10" box, Mattel, 1967 (fig. 5-17) . 75-135
Tin litho friction toy, armadillo-like
   dinosaur, lavender-gray, 1950s-1960s,
   Marx (fig. 5-18) 75-125
Tin litho friction toy, armored dinosaur,
   greenish, 1950s-1960s, Marx
   (see fig. 5-18) 75-125
Tin litho friction toy, Dimetrodon-like
   dinosaur without fin, 1950s-1960s,
   Marx (see fig. 5-18) 75-125
Tin litho friction toy, Protoceratops,
   lavender-gray, 1950s-1960s, Marx
   (see fig. 5-18) 75-125
Tin wind-up, Stegosaurus, tin litho with
   plastic fins, 8.5" long, boxed, China,
   Blic, 1990s (fig. 5-19) 8-15

Fig. 5-17: Mattel Strange Change Toy

Fig. 5-18: Marx tin litho dinosaurs

Fig. 5-20: Blic tin wind-up Tyrannosaurus

Fig. 5-19: Blic tin wind-up Stegosaurus

Fig. 5-21: Kenner Transformer

Tin wind-up, Tyrannosaurus, tin litho with
   plastic fins, 6", boxed, China, Blic, 1990s
   (fig. 5-20) $8-15
Transformer Dinobot, Grimlock,
   Tyrannosaurus, Kenner, 1985
   (fig. 5-21) 45-75
Transformer Dinobot, Slag, Triceratops,
   Kenner, 1985 45-75
Transformer Dinobot, Sludge, Brontosaurus,
   Kenner, 1985 45-75
Transformer Dinobot, Snarl, Stegosaurus,
   Kenner, 1985 45-75
Transformer Dinobot, Swoop, Pteranodon,
   Kenner, 1985 60-100
Wind-up toy, Caveman, boxed, "Y,"
   Japan, 1950s (fig. 5-22) 40-75
Wooden jointed Brontosaurus, TwisTum,
   1920s-1930s (fig. 5-23) 400-600
Wooden, jointed Brontosaurus, blue,
   unknown manufacturer, 1940s
   (fig. 5-24) 200-300

released. Also, the flying Quetzalcoatlus was completely repainted in a polka-dot camouflage that is a very rare variation of the original. These three figures came out near the end of the line's run and saw very limited distribution—they were primarily offered in the southeastern United States.

Largest of the figures are the huge Brontosaurus, motorized walking T-Rex and Triceratops, and non-motorized Diplodocus, Stegosaurus, and Torosaurus. The remaining figures are generally much smaller. Most attractive of all are some of these smaller dinosaurs, like the Struthiomimus, Protoceratops, Saurolophus, and Pachycephalosaurus. All of these figures were sold in boxed sets, complete with human or alien figures, battle weapons, armor, traps and equipment, instructions for assembly, and a small comic book containing dinosaur adventures. All of the figures had moveable arms and legs.

The popularity of the Dino-Riders toy line led to the creation of a Saturday morning cartoon show. Producer Jay Garfunkel created the show out of his love for dinosaurs. Garfunkel brought in Paul Kirchner as art director and designer. Popular author and dinosaur enthusiast Don Glut told us that he was a writer for the cartoon series, working with story editor Larry Parr. Glut said that they wrote standard characters and plots into scripts for each episode.

"It was very easy to write," Glut recalls, "And I could often write a complete episode in a day. We intentionally showed the toy products a lot in the cartoon. We would have the characters do outrageous things like having the Pachycephalosaurus bang its head against a rock to cause an earthquake."

Famous dinosaur expert and artist William Stout was on the payroll as an advisor for the TV show. He told us, "It was the classic situation. The producers always want a voice of authority for kids' shows— someone they can point to as an expert, giving the show validity. I got the job, but soon discovered it was a token position. I got credit for the show, but really didn't have much to do with what was used. I re-drew a few sheets they submitted, and I would suggest things like, 'This animal can't do what you are suggesting, but here's one that can.' They always thanked me and seemed to be taking my advice, but in the end, they never changed a thing."

Paleontologist Robert Bakker was an advisor for the Dino-Riders toy line. He left, however, after he told Tyco that designs for toys such as the

The Dino-Riders, Tyco's unique toy line, featured dinosaurs and space aliens.

Pachycephalosaurus and Stegosaurus were scientifically inaccurate, and was informed that no changes would be made.

"The Dino-Riders were the best action dinosaurs ever made," says Dr. Bakker. "Tyco used some really good artists. A couple of favorites of mine were the Pachycephalosaurus and Struthiomimus. The line was aimed at kids, but many of my adult colleagues would want to swipe some of the toys I kept in my office. I designed the Stegosaurus, and everyone liked it, except one marketing/publicity guy. He wanted to change the spikes to a massive size, bow out the legs, give it too many plates on its back —basically make it appear as Stegosaurus appeared back in old movies in the 1920s. I couldn't have my name associated with this design, and soon left the project."

Tyco also produced three video tapes for kids to enjoy, documenting the adventures of the Dino-Riders in the prehistoric era. The third adventure depicts the Dino-Riders and the Rulons doing battle in Earth's Ice Age, when the Dino-Riders accept the help of Neanderthal and Cro-Magnon humans, Woolly Mammoths, extinct wart hogs, ground sloths, and saber-toothed cats. Toys representing these animals, sold in 1990, were very well done, showing how the figures actually improved as the line progressed.

The first series of dinosaurs included Diplodocus, Deinonychus, Quetzalcoatlus, Styracosaurus, and a Pterodactyl. Each included a figure or two to ride each beast. The evil Rulons were packaged with the mighty T-Rex, Triceratops, another Deinonychus (the same figure as the one packaged with the Dino-

An evil Rulon riding a T-Rex fitted with a "brain box" battles the heroic Dino-Riders on the cover of this toy box.

Riders), Pteranodon, Monoclonius, and Ankylosaurus. Each dinosaur wore an array of removable armor plating and laser cannons or other weapons. Three of the Rulons' dinosaurs included traps to help catch and stop the Dino-Riders from escaping. One, two, or three Rulons were included with each dinosaur, depending on the size of the dinosaur. The T-Rex and Triceratops were battery-operated for motorized walking. Tyco seriously considered making the dinosaurs talk— both in the cartoon series and the toy line—but decided to stick with scientifically accurate animals.

The Dino-Rider and Rulon humanoid figures were also sold in carded two-packs, separate from their fighting dinosaurs. There were eight first-series and eight more second-series cards produced, with two figures on each. There were also six Dino-Rider Commandos released. Each card held one of these figures, plus fighting accessories.

The line was an immediate success, so more dinosaurs with figures were produced. The second series included a huge Brontosaurus that carried a squadron of flying Rhamphorhynchus bombers. Also in the second series were Torosaurus, Edmontonia, Stegosaurus, Pachycephalosaurus, Struthiomimus, Dimetrodon, and Protoceratops for the Dino-Riders. Added to the Rulon arsenal were a Saurolophus, Kentrosaurus, and Placerias.

A third and final series was started with the aforementioned Chasmosaurus, Pachyrhinosaurus, and revamped Quetzalcoatlus. The line's popularity had lost steam by this point, and no more pieces

were added. Few people wanted or even had the opportunity to buy these last three figures, and they are very desirable with collectors today. It was also about this time that the four prehistoric mammals were issued, plus six cards of Ice Age cavemen and aliens.

All of the Dino-Riders prehistoric animals have been carefully sculpted and usually utilized the latest scientific data of the day. Each was cast in hard plastic with some parts made of a softer vinyl. The air-brushed paint jobs on the toys were superb. Some of the video tapes sold in toy stores included a green, hard plastic, hollow T-Rex straddling the tape box. Marvel published a short-lived Dino-Rider comic book series. Fans could join the Dino-Riders Club by mailing in three Dino-Riders points (proof-of-purchase seals) and $3.50. Members received sixteen Dino-Riders collector's cards, a membership card, an iron-on emblem, and the official newsletter.

Even after the Dino-Riders series was gone, some of the identical prehistoric animal figures were re-released by Tyco for the Smithsonian Institution Collection Series and their comic-book-based "Cadillacs and Dinosaurs" line of toys. Not all of the dinosaurs were re-issued making those that were not potentially more collectible.

Merging dinosaurs and space aliens into a toy line worked well for Tyco for a time. The Dino-Rider toys were attractive, museum-quality pieces. While geared for children and rough play, they are also collectibles for all ages that will be desirable for years to come.

—Riff Smith and Mike Fredericks

DINO-RIDERS VALUE GUIDE

Ankylosaurus with Sting, first series,
   1988 (fig. D-1) $20-30
Brontosaurus with Ion, Serena, and Ayce,
   second series (figs. D-2 and D-3) 60-75
Chasmosaurus with Lava, third series,
   1990 (figs. D-4 and D-5) 80-120
Deinonychus (fig. D-6) with Rulon, dinotrap, first
   series, 1988 25-35
Deinonychus with Sky, first series,
   1988 20-30
Diplodocus (fig. D-7) with Questar, Mind-Zel, and

Fig. D-1: Ankylosaurus

Fig. D-4: Chasmosaurus

Fig. D-2: Brontosaurus with box

Fig. D-5: Rare Chasmosaurus mint in box

Fig. D-3: Brontosaurus with Dino-Riders and battle accessories

Fig. D-6: Deinonychus

Fig. D-7: Diplodocus

Fig. D-8: Dimetrodon

Fig. D-9: Edmontonia

Fig. D-10: Edmontonia with Axis box

Fig. D-11: Giant Ground Sloth

Fig. D-12: Kentrosaurus

Fig. D-13: Killer Wart Hog

Fig. D-14: Monoclonius

Fig. D-15: Pachyrhinosaurus

Aries, first series, 1988 35-45
Dimetrodon (fig. D-8) with Shado,
    second series $20-30
Edmontonia (fig. D-9) with Axis, second series
    (fig. D-10) 25-35
Giant Ground Sloth (fig. D-11) with Ulk,
    Neanderthal Caveman, Ice Age Series,
    1990 50-100
Kentrosaurus (fig. D-12) with Krok, second series
    25-35
Killer Wart Hog (fig. D-13) with Zar,
Cro-Magnon Caveman, Ice Age Series, 1990
    50-100
Monoclonius (fig. D-14) with Mako, Rulon,
    first series, 1988 20-30
Pachyrhinosaurus (fig. D-15) with Atlas,
    third series, 1990 80-120
Pachycephalosaurus (fig. D-16) with Togg,

Fig. D-16: Pachycephalosaurus

Fig. D-17: Placerias

Fig. D-18: Protoceratops

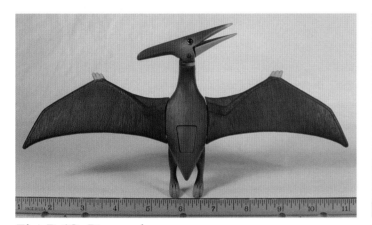

Fig. D-19: Pteranodon

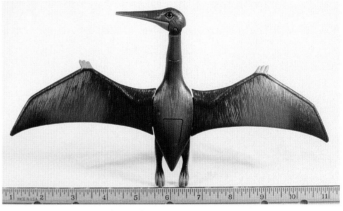

Fig. D-20: Pterodactyl

second series 25-35

Placerias (fig. D-17) with Skate,
second series $25-35

Protoceratops (fig. D-18) with Kanon,
second series 20-25

Pteranodon (fig. D-19) with Rasp, Rulon,
first series, 1988 20-25

Pterodactyl (fig. D-20) with Llahd,
first series, 1988 20-30

Quetzalcoatlus (fig. D-21) with Youngstar,
first series, 1988 20-30

Quetzalcoatlus (polka-dot version) (fig. D-22) with
Algar third series, 1990 80-120

Saber-Tooth Tiger (fig. D-23) with Kub,
Cro-Magnon Caveman, Ice Age Series,
1990 50-100

Saurolophus (fig. D-24) with Lokus,
second series 25-35

Stegosaurus (fig. D-25) with Vega and Tark, second

Fig. D-21: Quetzalcoatlus

Fig. D-22: Quetzalcoatlus, polka-dot version

Fig. D-23: Saber-Tooth Tiger

Fig. D-24: Saurolophus

Fig. D-25: Stegosaurus

Fig. D-26: Struthiomimus

Fig. D-29: Triceratops

Fig. D-27: Styracosaurus

Fig. D-30: Triceratops in box

Fig. D-28: Torosaurus

series 25-35
Struthiomimus (fig. D-26) with Nimbus, second
   series $25-35
Styracosaurus (fig. D-27) with Turret, first series,
   1988 25-35
Torosaurus (fig. D-28) with Gunner and Magnus,
   second series 30-35
Triceratops (figs. D-29 and D-30) with Hammerhead
   and Sidewinder, first series, 1988 40-55
Tyrannosaurus Rex with Krulos, Bitor,
   and Cobrus, first series, 1988
   (fig. D-31) 60-80
Woolly Mammoth (fig. D-32) with Grom, Neanderthal
   Caveman, Ice Age Series, 1990 50-100

Fig. D-31: Tyrannosaurus Rex

Fig. D-32: Woolly Mammoth

Figs. D-33 to D-36: Cavemen figures

Fig. 6-2: Movie poster, *Baby*

Fig. 6-1: Topps' candy container

MOVIE DINOSAURS

BABY . . . SECRET OF THE LOST LEGEND (1985)

Patrick McGoohan **(The Prisoner)**, William Katt, and Sean Young star in this Disney tale about dinosaurs found living in deepest Africa. A baby brontosaurus, coveted by the good guys and bad guys alike, is the movie's focus.

Candy containers, figural of Baby's head and
    full body, Topps, 1985, each (fig. 6-1) . . . $2-5
Movie poster, one-sheet, Disney, 1985
    (fig. 6-2) 8-15
Trading cards, Baby, Topps 1984
    Set of 66 cards, 11 stickers 8-12
    Unopened box 8-12

THE BEAST FROM 20,000 FATHOMS (1953)

Ray Harryhausen's first solo effort at stop-motion animation (after helping Willis O' Brien with **Mighty Joe Young**), was **The Beast from 20,000 Fathoms**. For it, he created the Rhedosaurus, a prehistoric creature thawed from its Arctic lair by an atomic bomb blast. Not only does this beast stomp through New York City, destroying people and property in its wake, it also spreads a fast-acting, lethal virus as it goes. The Coney Island amusement park climax is a highlight of dino-cinema.

Fig. 6-3: The Beast

Model kit, Rhedosaurus, with base,
    Action Hobbies $100-130
Model kit, large scale, paw raised,
    no base, Alternative Images 175-225
Model kit, the Beast, by Billiken, green
    vinyl, first issue, no base, 1980s 400-500
Model kit, the Beast, by Billiken, red
    vinyl, no base, 1980s (fig. 6-3) 350-400
Model kit, 13", resin, Pandemonium
    Productions, street scene base,
    unmarked 100-150
Model kit, 13.5", resin, The Resinator,
    rubble lighthouse base, unmarked . . 125-175

Fig. 6-4: Lunar Models' model kit

Fig. 6-5: T-Rex

Fig. 6-6: Window card, *Dinosaurus*

Monster Times, cover story, issue # 32 . . . $7-10
Monster Times, cover story, issue #44
   (poster inside) 15-20
Movie poster, one-sheet,
   Warner Brothers, 1953 350-550

CAVEMAN (1981)

Ringo Starr and Barbara Bach star in this stone age comedy. Also look for Shelley Long and Dennis Quaid.

Model kit, *Caveman* movie diorama
   with drunk T-Rex, Lunar Models
   (fig. 6-4) $100-140

DINOSAURUS (1960)

Lightning strikes, and a caveman who is thawed from his icy tomb befriends a young boy in this child-like fantasy offering. As the caveman is summarily confused by modern society and technology, the boy also pals around with a thawed brontosaurus, even managing to ride the thing.

   The lightning also manages to revive a tyrannosaurus, however, and the film's exciting climax features a fight between the T-Rex and a steam shovel. Must be seen to be believed.

Figurine, metal T-Rex with "Dinosaurus -
   Jack H. Harris" on its side, 2.5", 1960
   (fig. 6-5) $30-45
Model kit, Dinosaurus!, 1/50 scale,
   18" long, Lunar Models, 1990s 175-250

Movie poster, one-sheet,
   Universal-International, 1960 . . . . . . $50-80
Window card, *Dinosaurus,*
   Universal-International, 1960 (fig. 6-6) . 35-50

THE GIANT BEHEMOTH (1959)

This resurrected brontosaurus attacks England, moving in from a small coastal town to eventually trash London (two years before Gorgo). The dinosaur, animated by Willis O'Brien (**King Kong**) and others, also emits a cool-looking radioactive wave that can literally burn the skin off passersby. This is a good one.

Film, 8mm film, boxed, 400' (fig. 6-7) . . . $20-30
Model kit, with car in mouth, on city
   street base, Lunar Models (fig. 6-8) . . 125-175
Movie poster, one-sheet, Allied Artists,
   1959 50-85

Fig. 6-7: Film, *The Giant Behemoth*

Fig. 6-8: Lunar Models' model kit

Fig. 6-9: Comic book, *Gorgo*

Fig. 6-10: *Famous Monsters* magazine

Fig. 6-11: Lobby card, *Gorgo*

Fig. 6-12: Lobby card, *Gorgo*

Fig. 6-13: Alternative Images' model kit

Fig. 6-14: Mad Labs' model kit

Fig. 6-15: Movie poster, *Gorgo*

GORGO (1961)

In the late 1950s and early 1960s, a string of movies dealt with the notion of dinosaurs showing up in modern cities. London was visited by Gorgo, a gigantic prehistoric throwback with cute, wing-like ears and oversized clawed hands. **Gorgo** is really all about diligent parenting, as Mrs. Gorgo defies military assaults, wading up the Thames into the heart of London to rescue her baby from sideshow exploitation.

Gorgo collectibles tend to be expensive. The comic books frequently featured artwork by Steve Ditko, which increases demand among comic book collectors.

Comic book series, *Gorgo*, **Charlton, 1961-1965** (fig. 6-9)

#1	$70-170
#2	35-85
#3	35-85
#4-#10	20-50
#11-#16 (#12 has Reptisaurus [Reptilicus] crossover)	15-40
#17-#23	10-20

Comic book series, *Gorgo's Revenge/Return of Gorgo*, **Charlton, 1962-1963**

#1, *Gorgo's Revenge*, 1962	$15-35
#2-#3, *Return of Gorgo*	20-50
Comic book, *Fantastic Giants,* reprints original Gorgo and Konga comics, Charlton, 1966	20-50
Famous Monsters magazine, cover, issue #11	100-300
Famous Monsters magazine, cover (reprint of earlier cover art), issue #50 (fig. 6-10)	8-12
Lobby card, scene dependent, MGM, 1961, (fig. 6-11 and 6-12)	10-25
Model kit, resin, Gorgo stands over ruined buildings, Alternative Images (fig. 6-13)	125-175
Model kit, superdeformed Gorgo looks over shoulder, resin, Mad Labs (fig. 6-14)	15-25
Monster Times magazine, cover, issue no.12, 1970s	8-12
Movie poster, one-sheet, MGM, 1961 fig. 6-15)	75-150

Fig. 6-16: Book, *Movie Magic*

Fig. 6-17: *Famous Monsters* magazine

Fig. 6-18: Little Foot Brontosaurus

KING KONG (1933)

RKO's 1933 classic, **King Kong**, featured some of the earliest great dinosaur film footage. The ape and the dinosaurs were the creation of Willis O'Brien, the stop-motion animation pioneer who later guided young Ray Harryhausen through **Mighty Joe Young**.

Rather than attempting to list all King Kong collectibles here, we have selected a few with dinosaur tie-ins.

Board game, 10" x 20" box, Ideal, 1963 . $40-65
Board game, Milton Bradley, 1966 35-60
Book, *The Creation of Dino De Laurentiis'*
    King Kong, with photos, Pocket Books,
    1976 5-10
Book, *Great Monsters of the Movies*,
    Kong on cover, Pocket Books 8-12
Book, *Movie Magic*, Kong on cover,
    hardcover, St. Martins, 1974 (fig. 6-16) . 20-28
Cinefan magazine, cover, #1, 1974 15-20
Cinefex magazine, cover story,
    Willis O'Brien, issue #7, January 1982 .10-15
Famous Monsters magazine, cover story,
    issue #6 (fig. 6-17) 250-400
Famous Monsters magazine, cover story,
    issue #44 15-20
Famous Monsters magazine, cover story,
    issue #108, July 1974 20-30
King Kong magazine, Sportscene Publications,
    1977, with poster 15-25

Model kit, King Kong, Aurora, 10",
    1964 . . . .$75-400
Model kit, glow version, Aurora, 10",
    1969 75-250
Model kit, glow version, Aurora, 1972 . . . 75-175
Model kit, Dark Horse, 16.5", brown vinyl,
    RKO & Turner marks, rocky base 75-100
Model kit, Dark Horse, sculpted
    by Ray Harryhausen 115-155
Movie poster, *King Kong*, one-sheet,
    (Kong with Fay on left), 1933 . . 30,000-40,000
Movie poster, *King Kong*, one-sheet,
    1938 re-release 4,000-6,000
Movie poster, *King Kong*, one-sheet,
    1942 re-release 2,000-3,500
Movie poster, *King Kong*, one-sheet,
    duotone, 1947 re-release 250-400
Movie poster, *King Kong*, one-sheet,
    duotone, 1952 re-release 250-400
Movie poster, *King Kong*, one-sheet,
    1956 re-release (color) 300-500
Movie poster, *King Kong*, Kong holds
    Fay over city, smaller than one-sheet,
    Scala Film 25-50
Video, Deluxe 60th Anniversary Boxed Set
    with 4" Lucite film clip block 75-150
View-Master reel set 8-15
Watch, Deluxe boxed Fossil set with pewter
    figure, 1994 45-65

Fig. 6-19: Petrie Pterodactyl

Fig. 6-20: Cera Triceratops

Fig. 6-21: Duckie

Fig. 6-22: Little Foot

Fig. 6-23: Cera

Fig. 6-24: Sharp Tooth

Fig. 6-25: Spike

THE LAND BEFORE TIME (1988)

Don Bluth directed this animated dinosaur classic, which has spawned its own direct-to-video sequel empire. (Six titles exist at press time.) The original tells the story of five young dinosaurs on a survival trek to avoid extinction. Little Foot (a brontosaurus), and his friends Duckie (duckbill), Petrie (Pterodactyl), Spike (Ankylosaurus), and Cera (Triceratops) must also avoid the evil Sharp Tooth (a T-Rex, of course) on their journey to the Great Valley. This is a pretty neat film.

Burger King premium, Little Foot
   Brontosaurus, plastic wind-up walker,
   4.25" long, 1997 (fig. 6-18) $1-3
Burger King premium, Petrie Pterodactyl
   with flapping wings, plastic, 4.25", 1997
   (fig. 6-19) 1-3
Burger King premium, Cera Triceratops,
   rolling friction toy, plastic, 3.5" long, 1997
   (fig. 6-20) 1-3

Movie poster, one-sheet, 1988 . . . . $20-35
Movie poster, small video release promo,
   original title 5-10
Movie poster, video release promo,
   any sequel 4-8
Pizza Hut figure, Duckie, soft vinyl, 8",
   UCS & Amblin, 1988 (fig. 6-21) 2-4
Pizza Hut figure, Little Foot, soft vinyl, 8",
   UCS & Amblin, 1988 (fig. 6-22) 2-4
Pizza Hut figure, Cera, soft vinyl, 8",
   UCS & Amblin, 1988 (fig. 6-23) 2-4
Pizza Hut figure, Sharp Tooth, soft vinyl, 8",
   UCS & Amblin, 1988 (fig. 6-24) 2-4
Pizza Hut figure, Spike, soft vinyl, 8",
   UCS & Amblin, 1988 (fig. 6-25) 2-4
Trading Cards, *Land Before Time,*
   MCA Universal Home Video, 1997,
   mail-in offer, set of 8 cards 6-10

Fig. 6-26: Lobby card, *The Land Unknown*

Fig. 6-27: Film, *One Million B.C.*

Fig. 6-28: Film, *One Million Years B.C.*

THE LAND UNKNOWN (1957)

If you like cheesy dinosaurs, you'll love this B-movie classic. A navy helicopter lands in Antarctica only to find—surprise!—a hidden tropical area riddled with prehistoric beasts. William Reynolds, Shawn Smith, and Jock Mahoney star.

Lobby card, scene dependent, Universal-
  International, 1957 (fig. 6-26) $6-10
Movie poster, Universal-International, 1957 40-60

ONE MILLION B.C. (1940)

Victor Mature made his screen debut in this prehistoric epic, battling dinosaurs, volcanoes, and other prehistoric hazards alongside Carole Landis and Lon Chaney, Jr. It was the **Jurassic Park** of its day, with decorated lizards filmed in slow motion serving as the special effects. The dinosaur scenes, very convincing for the time, cropped up in numerous other genre films of the 1940s, 1950s, and 1960s.

Film, Super 8 film, boxed, Castle Films
  (fig. 6-27) $20-30

ONE MILLION YEARS B.C. (1966)

A Hammer Films classic, this not-to-be-missed dino pic featured the body of Raquel Welch and the stop-motion animation of Ray Harryhausen. What a combo. Raquel and Martine Beswick look so good in this one, no one seems to notice there's no dialogue whatsoever. There's a story in there somewhere about the Rock People fighting the Shell People, and

Fig. 6-29: *House of Hammer* magazine

the two tribes helping each other out in times of mutual danger. Raquel gets toted off by a Pterodactyl at one point. This may be the definitive stone-age drama.

Figure, Allosaurus, rubbery "synthetic
  flesh," by Jary Lesser, 1993 . . . . $35-50
Film, Super 8 film, selected scenes,
  boxed (fig. 6-28) 20-30
Magazine, *Castle of Frankenstein*,
  issue #12, cover story, 1960s 20-30

Fig. 6-31: Rex

Fig. 6-32: Rex puppet

Fig. 6-30: Monsters in Motion's model kit

Fig. 6-33: Walking Rex

TOY STORY - REX (1995)

What toy story is complete without a toy dinosaur?
Rex is the toy T-Rex that comes to life when no
one's looking, with the help of Wallace Shawn's
voice.

THE VALLEY OF GWANGI (1969)

One of the all-time-great dinosaur adventure movies,
The Valley of Gwangi features the fantastic stop-
motion animation of Ray Harryhausen. The story
was actually devised by King Kong animator Willis
O'Brien. James Franciscus plays a cowboy who dis-
covers a hidden desert valley in Mexico where prehistoric creatures still thrive.

Initially, Franciscus and his cowboy pals discov-
er a tiny eohippus, which is quickly bought by a
traveling circus. Eager for more adventure, the cow-
boys return to the prehistoric valley and manage to
lasso Gwangi, a giant carnivorous allosaurus-style
dinosaur. Brought back to the Mexican village on
display, Gwangi soon breaks loose, terrorizes the
populace, and finally crashes into a church, where
he is symbolically killed in a fiery conflagration.
Great, great stuff.

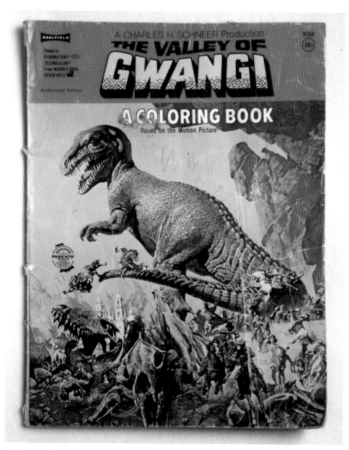

Fig. 6-34: Coloring book

Fig. 6-36: Eel Factory's model kit

Fig. 6-37: Monsters in Motion's model kit

Fig. 6-35: Comic book, *The Valley of Gwangi*

Fig. 6-38: Film, *When Dinosaurs Ruled the Earth*

Fig. 6-39: Lunar Models' model kit

Fig. 6-40: Lobby card, *When Women Had Tails*

Great, great stuff.
Coloring book, Saalfield, 1969
    (fig. 6-34) $30-50
Comic book, *The Valley of Gwangi*,
    Dell Movie Classic, December 1969
    (fig. 6-35) 35-75
Model kit, Gwangi vs. Triceratops, resin,
    by Mike Evans, Alchemy Works 150-200
Model kit, Gwangi on rock base with
    name plate, resin, Eel Factory
    (fig. 6-36) 100-120
Model kit, Gwangi, sculpted by Joe Laudati,
    Monsters in Motion (fig. 6-37) 100-200

Model kit, Gwangi roped by cowboy, 10",
    Resin from the Grave, 1992 . . . . . . $125-175
Model kit, superdeformed, by Eel Factory,
    3", resin, unmarked 65-85
Movie poster, one-sheet, Warner Brothers,
    1969 75-150
Soundtrack CD, classic film music of
    Jerome Moross 12-15

WHEN DINOSAURS RULED THE EARTH (1969)

This Hammer Films classic starred Victoria Vetri, Robin Hawdon, and Patrick Allen. Written by J. G. Ballard, with effects by Jim Danforth, this one was certainly inspired by the success of Hammer's earlier Raquel Welch vehicle, **One Million Years B.C.**

Film, Super 8, Warner Brothers, boxed
    (fig. 6-38) $15-25
Model kit, "When Dinosaurs Ruled . . ."
    with Chasmosaurus, 13" x 5", Lunar
    Models (fig. 6-39) 150-200
Movie poster, Hammer Films, 1969 45-75

WHEN WOMEN HAD TAILS (1970)

Senta Berger stars in this bawdy Italian prehistoric offering. She enters the lives of a small group of cave-bachelors and, together, they learn about the differences between the sexes. It's billed as a comedy, but rated "R," like its 1971 sequel, **When Women Lost Their Tails.**

Lobby card, scene dependent, 1970
    (fig. 6-40) $5-10
Movie poster, 1970 35-50

JURASSIC PARK
AND JURASSIC PARK:
THE LOST WORLD

Fig. J-1: Looking real as life! Kenner's *Jurassic Park* T-Rex

Like nearly every boy who grew up in the 1950s and 1960s, Stephen Spielberg loved dinosaurs. Unlike the other boys, however, Spielberg got the chance to display some of his dinosaur passion on the big screen, in the blockbuster hit **Jurassic Park** (1993) and its sequel, **The Lost World** (1997).

Jurassic Park tells the story of an eccentric millionaire who decides to create a dinosaur theme park, using live cloned dinosaurs as his main attraction. He buys an island, hires some scientists, and makes his dream come true. Just before the park is set to open, he calls in a team of various experts (bankers, scientists, and dinosaur specialists) to see his amazing accomplishment.

As we all know by now, "chaos theory" prevails; the dinosaurs run amok, people get chomped, and the park never opens to the public. Instead, the island,

Fig. J-2: *Jurassic Park* action figures with "Attacking Jaws" and "Slashing Jaws"

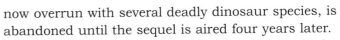

Fig. J-3: *J-P* fans who purchased a screaming Dino got a collector card!

Fig. J-4: 3-D Pop-Out Set

now overrun with several deadly dinosaur species, is abandoned until the sequel is aired four years later.

The sequel seemed to lose a lot of the punch of the original, although the scenes of the T-Rex prowling through San Diego were memorable.

Jurassic Park set a new standard for dinosaurs on film. The dinosaurs were breathtaking, looking every bit as real as the human actors and actresses. Showcasing such popular childhood species as Tyrannosaurus Rex and Triceratops, it also made the Velociraptor a household name.

Jurassic Park also had a incredible impact on dinosaur collectibles (figs. J-1-J-3) as the film's phenomenal popularity inspired thousands of dinosaur-related objects.

—Dana Cain

3-D Pop-Out Set, craft toy, shown in French
  packaging, 1990s (fig. J-4) $4-8

Action figures and accessories, **Jurassic Park,**
Kenner, Series 1, 1993

Alan Grant, 5" $6-12
Coelophysis Swarm (pair), Dino-Strike
  series, 7.5" long (figs. J-5 and J-6) 10-18
Command Compound Playset,
  electronic 75-100
Dennis Nedry, 5" 8-15
Dilophosaurus, "Spitter" with Venom Spray,
  with Capture Gear, 8.5" long
  (figs. J-7 and J-8) 6-12
Dilophosaurus, DinoScreams series 12-20
Dimetrodon, Dino-Strike series, green, 7.5"
  (fig. J-9). 6-12
Ellie Sattler, 5" 10-15
Pteranodon, Dino-Strike series, 9" across
  (fig. J-10) 6-12
Robert Muldoon, 5 5-10
Stegosaurus, Giant Attack Size Dinosaur . 30-50
Tim Murphy, 5" 5-10

Fig. J-5: Kenner's Coelophysis Swarm (pair), in blister pack

Fig. J-6: Coelophysis Swarm, unpackaged

Fig. J-7: Kenner's Dilophosaurus, "Spitter" with Venom Spray and Capture Gear

Fig. J-8: Kenner's Dilophosaurus, "Spitter," unpackaged

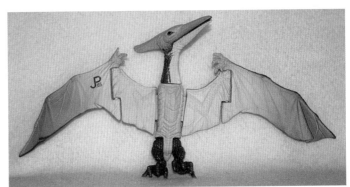

Fig. J-9: Dino-Strike series Dimetrodon

Fig. J-10: Dino-Strike series Pteranodon

Fig. J-11: Kenner's Triceratops, Giant Attack Size Dinosaur, with removable wound

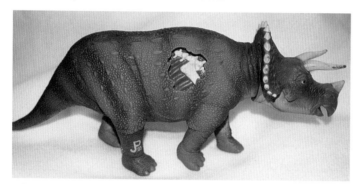

Fig. J-12: Triceratops with wound, unboxed

Fig. J-13: Boxed, 24" T-Rex, from Kenner

Fig. J-14: Unboxed Kenner T-Rex

Fig. J-15: Bush Devil Tracker vehicles

Fig. J-16: Jungle Explorer

Action figures and accessories, **Jurassic Park,**
Kenner, Series 2, 1994

Fig. J-17: Dino-Strike series Pachycephalosaurus

Fig. J-18: Quetzalcoatlus with capture gear

Fig. J-19: Dino-Strike series Tanystropheus

Fig. J-20: Utahraptor "Ripper"

Fig. J-21: Young T-Rex

Fig. J-22: Ajay, Big Game Stalker

Fig. J-23: Junior T-Rex with broken leg and healing cast

Action figures and accessories, **Jurassic Park: The Lost World,** *Kenner, 1997*

Fig. J-24: Junior T-Rex, unpackaged

Fig. J-27: Steel Beak, the Giant Pteranodon

Fig. J-25: Nick Van Owen, Video Expert—without hat and with hat

Fig. J-28: Steel Jaw, the Baryonyx

Fig. J-29: *Jurassic Park* Dinosaur Bubble Bath

Fig. J-26: Slice, the Spinosaurus

Fig. J-30: Jurassic Park Deluxe Play Set

Fig. J-31: *Lost World* Dinosaur Costume

Fig. J-32: Costume, *Lost World* Staff (male)

Mobile Command Center Playset $40-60
Nick Van Owen (with or without hat), 5",
 Series 1 or 2 (fig. J-25) 3-6
Peter Ludlow, 5", Series 1 3-6
Plateface, electronic, Attack Roar series . . 15-25
Ram Head, Dino-Strike series 15-25
Raptor, 5", Series 1 4-8
Raptor, Hatchling series 6-12
Roland Tembo (with or without hair), 5",
 Series 1 3-6
Sarah Harding, 5", Series 1 5-10
Slice, the Spinosaurus, electronic, Attack
 Roar series (fig. J-26) 5-10
Snap-Jaw, electronic, Attack Roar series . 15-25
Spike Tail, Dino-Strike series 15-25
Steel Beak, boxed Giant Pteranodon
 (fig. J-27) 15-25
Steel Jaw, Baryonyx, 5", Series 2 (fig. J-28) . 4-8
T-Rex, Hatchling series 6-12
Thrasher T-Rex, boxed dinosaur 15-25
Triceratops, Hatchling series 6-12
Trike, Series 1 or 2 4-8
Vehicle, D.A.R.T., with Roland Tembo 8-15
Vehicle, Dino-Snare Dirt Bike, with Carter . 6-12
Vehicle, Glider Pack, with Malcolm 5-10
Vehicle, Ground Tracker 8-15
Vehicle, High Hide, with Van Owen 8-15
Vehicle, Humvee 15-25
Vehicle, Net Trapper 8-15

Action figures and accessories, **Jurassic Park, Chaos Effect**, *Kenner, 1998*

Ian Malcolm, 5" $5-10
Roland Tembo, 5" 5-10
Ultimasaurus 6-12
Vehicle, Air S.A.B.R.E. with Dieter Stark . . 5-10
Vehicle, Land S.A.B.R.E. with Eddie Carr . . 5-10
Velociraptryx 6-12

Bubble Bath, *Jurassic Park* Dinosaur
 Bubble Bath, with figural top, plastic
 bottle (fig. J-29) $5-8
Colorforms, *Jurassic Park* Deluxe Play Set,
 Colorforms, 1993 (fig. J-30) 7-10
Costume, *Lost World* Dinosaur, 1997
 (fig. J-31)   6-12
Costume, *Lost World* Staff, 1997
 (figs. J-32 and J-33) 5-10
Cup, *Jurassic Park*, McDonald's, plastic
 with full color wrap graphics, 6.5" tall,
 6 designs, each (figs. J-34 through J-39) . 1-3

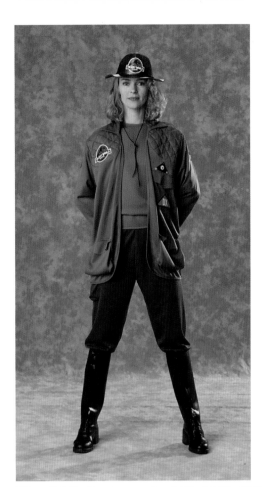

Fig. J-33: Costume, *Lost World* Staff (female)

Figs. J-34 through J-39: McDonald's *Jurassic Park* plastic cups

Fig. J-40: Diecast figures, *The Lost World*

Fig. J-41: Diecast Ankylosaurus

Fig. J-42: Diecast Dimetrodon

Fig. J-43: Diecast Gallimimus

Fig. J-44: Diecast Plesiosaur

Fig. J-45: Diecast Tyrannosaurus

Diecast figures, **The Lost World,** *miniature, painted figurines on bases, UCS & Amblin, 1993*
These were originally sold in 2-packs, with two movie collector trading cards included. (Fig. J-40)

Ankylosaurus (fig. J-41) $4-8
Dimetrodon (fig. J-42) 4-8
Gallimimus (fig. J-43) 4-8
Plesiosaur (fig. J-44) 4-8
Tyrannosaurus (fig. J-45) 4-8

Dino Sound Target Set, *Jurassic Park,*
   set with toy dart guns, etc. 8-12
Eraser, *Lost World* Triceratops, carded
   (fig. J-46) 2-4
Eraser, *Lost World* T-Rex, on card
   (see fig. J-46) 2-4
Eraser, *Lost World* Velociraptor, on card
   (see fig. J-46) 2-4

Figures, plastic miniatures,
average 3" tall, Dakin, 1992

Brachiosaurus (fig. J-47) $3-6
Gallimimus (fig. J-48) 3-6
Frilled Spitter (fig. J-49) 3-6
Triceratops (fig. J-50) 3-6
Tyrannosaurus, adult (fig. J-51) 3-6
Velociraptor (fig. J-52) 3-6

Game, *Jurassic Park* Game, with extra-large
   board, 16 dinosaur figures,
   Milton Bradley $15-25
Key chain, *Lost World,* Parasauralophus,
   with sound, carded 3-5
Key chain, *Lost World* T-Rex, with sound,
   carded 3-5
Key chain, *Lost World,* Velociraptor, with
   sound, carded 3-5
Liquid Soap, *Jurassic Park* Dinofoam Soap,
   squirts from figural dino head top 5-8

Fig. J-46: *Lost World* erasers

Fig. J-51: Adult Tyrannosaurus, by Dakin

Fig. J-47: Brachiosaurus, by Dakin

Fig. J-52: Velociraptor

Fig. J-48: Gallimimus

Fig. J-49: Frilled Spitter, by Dakin

Fig. J-50: Triceratops, by Dakin

Fig. J-53: *Jurassic Park,* red plastic lunchbox and thermos, with decal

Fig. J-54: *Lost World* red plastic lunch kit, by Thermos

Fig. J-55: Magic Rocks

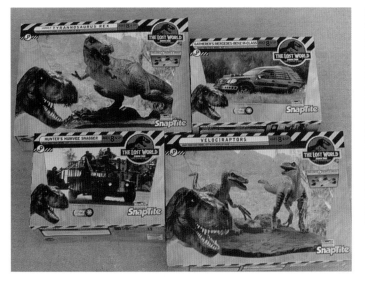

Fig. J-57: Spitter model kit, by Lindberg

Fig. J-56 (top left): *Lost World* Tyrannosaurus Rex model kit, by Revell
Fig. J-56 (bottom right): Model kit, *Lost World* Velociraptors
Fig. J-56 (top right): Model kit, *Lost World* Mercedes-Benz
Fig. J-56 (bottom left): Model kit, *Lost World* Hunter's Humvee Snagger

Model kit, Brachiosaurus, 1/19,
   Horizon $100-135
Model kit, Hadrosaurus (Corythosaurus),
   Lindberg, 1993 10-15
Model kit, *Lost World* Tyrannosaurus Rex,
   snap-together, 1/25 scale, Revell,
   (fig. J-56, top left) 10-15
Model kit, *Lost World* Velociraptors,
   snap-together, 1/25 scale, Revell
   (fig. J-56, bottom right) 10-15
Model kit, *Lost World* vehicle,
   Mercedes-Benz, snap-together, Revell
   (fig. J-56, top right) 7-10
Model kit, *Lost World* vehicle, Hunter's
   Humvee Snagger, snap-together, Revell
   (fig. J-56, bottom left) 7-10
Model kit, Spitter (Dilophosaurus),
   Horizon, 1990s 80-110
Model kit, Spitter, Lindberg, 1993
   (fig. J-57) 15-22
Model kit, Stegosaurus, Lindberg, 1993
   (fig. J-58) 10-15
Model kit, Tyrannosaurus, Horizon,
   1990s (fig. J-59) 100-135
Model kit, Tyrannosaurus, Lindberg,
   1993 20-25
Model kit, Tyrannosaurus Rex, 1/24 scale
   PVC kit, Tsukuda Hobby, Japan
   fig. J-60) 80-120

Fig. J-58: Stegosaurus model kit, by Lindberg

Fig. J-59: Tyrannosaurus model kit, by Horizon

Fig. J-60: Tyrannosaurus Rex model kit from Tsukuda Hobby

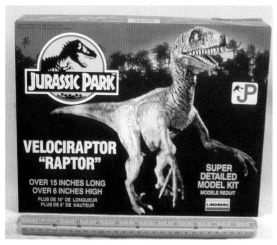

Fig. J-61: Velociraptor model kit, by Lindberg

Fig. J-62: *Jurassic Park* pinball game

Fig. J-63: *Jurassic Park* full-size pinball machine

Fig. J-64: *Jurassic Park* Play House

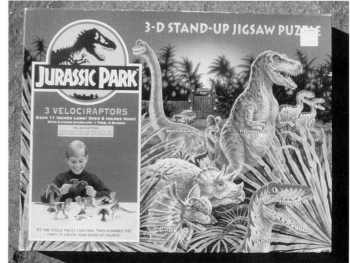

Fig. J-65: 3-D stand-up jigsaw puzzle

Fig. J-66: Stegosaurus remote control toy

Fig. J-67: Hollow plastic sign

Fig. J-68: Topps *Jurassic Park* trading card

Radio Control Truck with Spitting Dilopho-
saurus, *Lost World*, Tyco, 1997 . . . . . . $20-30
Remote Control toy, *Lost World*, Mercedes
Benz AAV, Toy Biz, 1997 15-25
Remote Control toy, *Lost World*,
Pachycephalosaurus, Toy Biz, 1997 . . . 15-30
Remote Control toy, *Lost World*,
Stegosaurus, Toy Biz, 1997 (fig. J-66) . . . 8-15
Remote Control toy, *Lost World*, Triceratops,
Toy Biz, 1997 8-15
Remote Control toy, *Lost World*,
Tyrannosaurus Rex, Toy Biz, 1997 15-30
Sign, hollow plastic, display item with logo,
1990s (fig. J-67) 15-25
Slot Car set, *Jurassic Park* Survival Chase,
Tyco, 1990s 20-30
Slot Car set, *Lost World* Electric Race Set,
Tyco, 1990s 15-25

TRADING CARDS

Jurassic Park *(series 1 or series 2), Topps, 1993 (fig. J-68)*

Full set (Series 1 has 88 cards, 11 stickers;
Series 2 has 66 cards, 11 stickers),
each $10-15
Hologram card (4 different; same 4 in
each series), each 5-8
Unopened box 25-30

Trading Cards, **Jurassic Park** *Gold, Topps, 1993*

Set of 88 cards, 10 art cards $25-30
Hologram card (4 different; same as in
regular series, with different numbers),
each 7-10
Unopened box 55-70

Fig. J-69: Topps *Jurassic Park* trading card

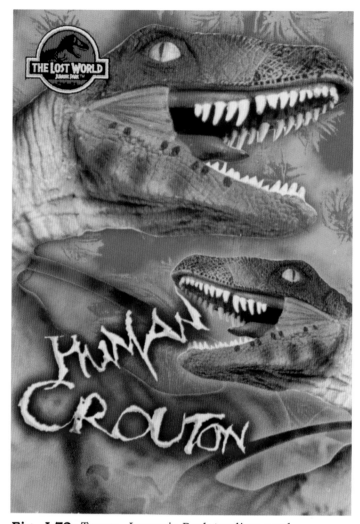

Fig. J-70: Topps *Jurassic Park* trading card

Fig. J-72: Topps *Jurassic Park* trading card

Fig. J-73: Topps *Jurassic Park* trading card

Fig. J-74: Topps *Jurassic Park* trading card

Fig. J-71: Topps *Jurassic Park* trading card

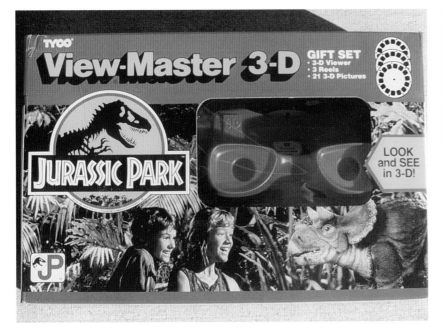

Fig. J-75: View-Master 3-D Gift Set

Fig. J-76: *Lost World* Virtual Pet

Trading Cards, **Jurassic Park:
The Lost World,** *Topps, 1997*

Set of 72 cards, 11 stickers $14-18
Unopened box (figs. J-68–J-74) 30-35

View-Master 3-D Gift Set, *Jurassic Park,*
   with viewer and 3 reels (fig. J-75) . . . . .$ 5-10
Virtual Pet, *Lost World,* Baby T-Rex Giga
   Pet, carded (fig. J-76) 8-15
Watch, *Lost World* with T-Rex head over
   dial face, 1997 (fig. J-77) 10-15

Fig. J-77: *Lost World* watch

Baby Sinclair

Fig. 7-1: Barney

TV DINOSAURS

BARNEY AND FRIENDS (1992–PRESENT)

The most obvious thing to say about this PBS character is: you either love him or you hate him. Barney is a stuffed dinosaur who comes to life and plays with children, singing songs, and, of course, learning positive life lessons along the way. His popularity with the pre-school set is unparalleled.

Barney is actually the brainchild of Sheryl Leach, who was looking for something to amuse her son when she created the character back in 1988. An ambitious mother, she wound up scripting and producing three videos about "Barney and the Backyard Gang" starring Sandy Duncan.

PBS eventually took note of **Barney** and began producing the series in the early 1990s.

Bank, figural vinyl, Barney with backpack,
    waving, 7", REI, 1992 (fig. 7-1) $3-5
Lunchbox, Barney & Baby Bop, purple plastic
    with decal, Thermos, 1992 (fig. 7-2) 4-8
Lunchbox, Barney & Baby Bop, blue plastic
    with decal, Thermos, 1993 (fig. 7-3) 4-8
Model kit, Barney vs. Velociraptor, by John
    Fischner for Dreamstar Productions,
    1990s 200-300

Fig. 7-2: Purple Barney & Baby Bop lunchbox

Fig. 7-3: Blue Barney & Baby Bop lunchbox

Fig. 7-4: Barney vs. Velociraptor

Fig. 7-5: Earl Sinclair

Fig. 7-6: Fran Sinclair

Fig. 7-7: Charlene Sinclair

DINOSAURS (1991-1994)

Meet the Sinclairs, a family reminiscent of many other classic TV families, except for one thing—they're all talking dinosaurs. Earl Sinclair, a Megalosaurus, is married to Fran. They have three kids—a teenage boy named Robbie, a twelve-year-old daughter named Charlene, and, of course, Baby. Fun ensues as the Sinclairs and their dinosaur friends gradually move toward extinction.

The show featured quite ambitious special effects, and merged the talents of Walt Disney Television, Jim Henson Productions, and Michael Jacobs Productions. It was actually all live action, with actors inside the complex dinosaur suits, and facial expressions created by "audio animatronics."

Action Figures, 5", Hasbro, 1990s

Earl Sinclair (fig. 7-5)	$8-12
Fran Sinclair (fig. 7-6)	8-12
Charlene Sinclair (fig. 7-7)	8-12
Robbie Sinclair (fig. 7-8)	8-12
Baby Sinclair (with meat bottle) (fig. 7-9)	8-12
B.D. Richfield (Earl's boss) (fig. 7-10)	8-12

Action Figures, fast food premiums, 3", 1990s

Earl Sinclair in hard hat (fig. 7-11)	$2-4
Fran Sinclair in apron (fig. 7-12)	2-4
Charlene Sinclair with phone (fig. 7-13)	2-4
Robbie Sinclair with guitar (fig. 7-14)	2-4
Baby Sinclair with sucker (fig. 7-15)	2-4
Baby Sinclair in egg (fig. 7-16)	2-4
Grandma Ethyl in rocking chair (fig. 7-17)	2-4

Fig. 7-8: Robbie Sinclair

Fig. 7-9: Baby Sinclair

Fig. 7-10: B.D. Richfield

Fig. 7-11: Earl Sinclair

Fig. 7-12: Fran Sinclair

Fig. 7-13: Charlene Sinclair

Fig. 7-14: Robbie Sinclair

Fig. 7-15: Baby Sinclair with sucker

Fig. 7-16: Baby Sinclair in egg

Fig. 7-17: Grandma Ethyl

THE FLINTSTONES (1960-1994)

The Flintstones was TV's first prime-time cartoon series. Created by Joseph Hanna and William Barbera (Hanna-Barbera), the series ran for six years in prime time in the 1960s, before shifting to a Saturday morning rerun schedule. During the 1970s and early 1980s, the Flintstones were featured in several short-lived series, including **The Flintstones Comedy Hour**, **The Flintstones Show**, **The New Fred and Barney Show**, **Fred and Barney Meet the Thing**, **Fred and Barney Meet the Schmoo**, **The Flintstones Comedy Show**, and **Flintstone Funnies**. Finally, the characters found another successful venue, with **The Flintstone Kids**, a Saturday morning series which aired in the late 1980s and early 1990s.

More recently, a live action Flintstones film was produced, starring John Goodman and Rosie O'Donnell, among others.

Originally, **The Flintstones** was a thinly veiled animated version of **The Honeymooners**. Fred and Wilma Flintstone and their best friends Barney and Betty Rubble live in Bedrock. Fred likes to bowl and frequently gets in trouble with his wife and his boss for various indiscretions. Wilma and Betty fret over their husbands' shortcomings and plot to get even with them. Eventually, both couples decide to breed, and the adorable Pebbles Flintstone and the irrepressible Bamm-Bamm Rubble are introduced.

The Flintstones have a pet dinosaur, named Dino, who barks and acts like a big dog, while the Rubbles own Baby Puss, a saber-toothed house cat. One of the coolest things about the Flintstones is their prehistoric gadgetry: the Woolly Mammoth trunk shower head, the hungry dinosaur disposal, the pterodactyl beak stereo arm and needle, etc.

An incredible array of Flintstones memorabilia has been produced over the past forty years or so.

Fig. 7-18: Flintstones Bedrock City postcard

FLINTSTONES BEDROCK CITY
Custer, South Dakota

Fans and collectors of The Flintstones will want to plan a trip to Custer, South Dakota, to visit the Hanna-Barbera-licensed theme park, Flintstones Bedrock City. It's near Mt. Rushmore, in an area that is rife with fabulous family tourist attractions. The Bedrock City gift shop has a great selection of Flintstones items not available anywhere else. And the park doesn't deal with mail order—you just have to go there and check it out!

Also at Bedrock City, you can ride the Flintmobile, munch on Brontoburgers and Dino dogs, watch Flintstones cartoons at the Rockmore Theater, and peek into the windows of the life-size buildings. (See what really goes on in Fred and Wilma's bedroom.)

There's also a train ride and fully-equipped camping grounds. It's a great time all round, with a rare opportunity to scoop up some truly unique Flintstones memorabilia (**fig. 7-18**).

Action figures, Flintstones, Mattel, 1993-1994 (from live action film)

Betty & Bamm-Bamm, 5", carded	$5-10
Big Bite Fred, deluxe figure	5-10
Big Shot Fred, 5", carded	5-10
Bowl-O-Rama Fred, deluxe figure	5-10
Cliff Vandercave, 5", carded	5-10
Crash Test Barney, deluxe figure	5-10
Dino, 5", carded	5-10
Fillin' Station Barney, 5", carded (fig. 7-19)	5-10
Hard Hat Fred, 5", carded	5-10
Lawn Mowin' Barney, 5", carded	5-10
Vehicle, Flintmobile	15-25
Vehicle, Le Sabre 5000	15-25
Wilma & Pebbles, 5", carded (fig. 7-20)	5-10
Yabba-Dabba-Doo Fred, large figure	10-20

Action figures, Flintstones Kids, 5" figures, Coleco, 1987-1988

Barney, Series 1, 1987	$8-15
Betty, Series 1, 1987	8-15
Dino, Series 1, 1987	8-15
Fang, Series 1, 1987	8-15
Freddy, Series 1, 1987	5-10
Wilma, Series 1, 1987	8-15
Bedrock Airlines, Series 1, 1987	15-25
Bedrock Elementary, Series 1, 1987	15-30
Bedrock Firefighter, Series 1, 1987	8-15

Fig. 7-19: Mattel's Fillin' Station Barney

Fig. 7-22: Barney, bendable figure

Fig. 7-23: Betty, bendable figure

Fig. 7-24: Dino, bendable figure

Fig. 7-25: Fred, bendable figure

Fig. 7-20: Mattel's Wilma & Pebbles

Fig. 7-21: Bamm-Bamm, bendable figure

Fig. 7-26: Pebbles, bendable figure

Fig. 7-27: Wilma, bendable figure

Bendable figures, 4.5″, JusToys

Fig. 7-28: Fred riding Dino the Dinosaur

Fig. 7-29: Dinosaur cereal premiums

Fig. 7-30: Bamm-Bamm doll

Ashtray, Wilma embossed on ceramic oval,
  1960 . . . . $20-30
Bank, large figural chalkware, Barney or
  Fred 60-85
Bank, figural Dino with golf bag, made
  in China, 8.5" tall 75-100
Bank, "Fred Loves Wilma," 8" tall, ceramic,
  1960s 65-95
Bank, Barney with Bamm-Bamm, plastic
  figural, 19", 1971 15-30
Battery-Op toy, Fred Riding Dino the
  Dinosaur, 12" tall, fur-coated tin,
  Marx, 1962 (fig. 7-28) 250-400
Battery-Op toy, Fred Flintstone's Bedrock
  Band, tin litho and plush/vinyl, ALPS,
  1962 300-450
Beach ball, inflatable, with Flintstones
  graphics, 1973 10-20
Bedrock Express, wind-up toy, track
  through Bedrock, wind-up plastic
  hand car, Marx, 1962 175-250
Cereal premiums, colorful plastic dinosaurs,
  from Pebbles Cereal, 1980s, each
  (fig. 7-29) 2-5
Coloring book, "The Flintstones," Whitman,
  1960 15-25

Costume, Fred Flintstone, Ben Cooper,
  1962 . . . . $30-45
Doll, Baby Pebbles, 16" tall, leopard-print
  outfit, bone in hair, Ideal, 1962 125-200
Doll, Bamm-Bamm, 17" tall, Ideal #BB17,
  1962 (fig. 7-30) 75-150
Doll, Pebbles Flintstone, cloth body with
  vinyl head, arms, and legs, 12", Mighty
  Star, 1982 25-40
Doll, Pebbles and Her Cradle, 12" doll with
  plastic log cradle, boxed, Ideal, 1964 . 175-300
Doll, Tiny Bamm-Bamm, 12" tall, in
  window box, Ideal, 1963 80-150
Doll, Tiny Pebbles, 12" tall, in window
  box, Ideal, 1964 85-160
Figure, Baby Puss, soft vinyl, 10",
  in window box, Knickerbocker, 1961 . . 75-125
Figure, Dino, plastic, 8", Dakin, 1970 40-60
Figure, Fred, soft vinyl, 15",
  in window box, Knickerbocker, 1960 . . . 20-30
Figure, Fred, hollow plastic, 5.5", painted
  (fig. 7-31) 5-8
Figure, Fred, vinyl with cloth outfit, 8",
  Dakin, 1970 (fig. 7-32) 15-30
Figures, Fred, Barney, Wilma, or Betty,
  colored plastic, 3", Empire, 1976, each . 15-25

Fig. 7-31: Fred figure, hollow plastic

Fig. 7-32: Fred figure, vinyl with cloth

Fig. 7-33: Barney in car

Fig. 7-34: Dino riding scooter

Fig. 7-35: Fred in car

Fig. 7-36: Pebbles and Bamm-Bamm in wagon

Fig 7-37: Wilma in car

Fig. 7-38: Bamm-Bamm riding green dinosaur

Fig. 7-39: Barney riding Dino

Fig. 7-40: Betty riding blue dinosaur

Fig. 7-41: Dino riding Woolly Mammoth

Fig. 7-42: Fred riding green turtle

Fig. 7-43: Pebbles riding Triceratops

Figures, all on wheeled vehicles, 2-3",
Applause, 1980s-1990s

Barney (fig. 7-33) $1-3
Dino (fig. 7-34) 1-3
Fred (fig. 7-35) 1-3
Pebbles and Bamm-Bamm (fig. 7-36) 1-3
Wilma (fig. 7-37) 1-3

Figures, Denny's Restaurants, 2-3",
promotional toys

Bamm-Bamm riding green dinosaur
 (fig. 7-38) $2-5
Barney riding Dino (fig. 7-39) 2-5
Betty riding blue dinosaur (fig. 7-40) 2-5
Dino riding Woolly Mammoth (fig. 7-41) 2-5
Fred riding green turtle (possibly an
 Ankylosaurus) (fig. 7-42) 2-5
Pebbles riding Triceratops (fig. 7-43) 2-5

Fig. 7-44: Denny's Flintstones lunchbox

Fig. 7-45: Aladdin's Flintstones lunchbox, front

Fig. 7-46: Aladdin's Flintstones lunchbox, back

Fig. 7-47: Dino, McDonald's premium

Fig. 7-48: Dino Pez dispenser

Fig. 7-49: Bedrock City souvenir plate

Friction car, Wilma drives, tin litho with
soft vinyl head, 3.5" tall, Marx, 1962 . $50-100

Game, Flintstones Brake-Ball Game,
Whitman, 1960 30-45

Game, Flintstones Cut-Ups Game,
Whitman, 1962 35-50

Game, Dino the Dinosaur Game,
Transogram, 1961 40-65

Game, Flintstones Stone Age Game,
Transogram, 1961 30-50

Game, Flintstones Hoppy the
Hopparoo Game, Transogram, 1965 . . 75-100

Game, Flintstones Mechanical Shooting
Gallery Target Game, 14", tin litho,
Marx, 1962 200-275

Game, Flintstone Prehistoric Animal Rummy,
3.5" x 3.5" box, Ed-U-Card, 1960 25-40

Give-A-Show Projector Set, Flintstones on
box, (other Hanna-Barbera sets also),
Kenner, 1963 40-60

Great Big Punchout Book, 11" x 22",
paper doll book, Whitman, 1961 25-40

Juice glass, from jelly, several designs,
1960s, each 3-6

Lamp, plastic figural Fred base with
characters on shade, 1961 85-135

Lunchbox, The Flintstones, Denny's
restaurants, red plastic with decal
(fig. 7-44) 12-20

Lunchbox, The Flintstones and Dino,
steel, Aladdin, 1962
(figs. 7-45 and 7-46) 150-225

Lunchbox, Pebbles and Bamm-Bamm,
vinyl, Aladdin, 1971 75-125

Lunch kit thermos, first issue—orange,
Aladdin, 1962 30-35

Lunch kit thermos, second issue—yellow,
Aladdin, 1963 25-30

McDonald's premium, Dino figure, live
action film tie-in, 1987 (fig. 7-47) 1-3

Paper dolls, Pebbles and Bamm-Bamm,
Whitman, 1965 20-30

Pez dispenser, Dino, 4.5" (fig. 7-48) 3-5

Pillowcase, shows Fred at Piano, 1960 . . . 20-30

Plate, Flintstone's Bedrock City souvenir,
9" across, Custer, South Dakota,
1990s (fig. 7-49) 10-16

Playset, Bedrock Village, TV Tinykins,
Marx playset #5948, 1962 400-650

Playset, Flintstones, TV Tinykins, smaller
versions, 1960s 75-150

Playset, Flintstones Hunting Party,
with 3 dinosaurs, Marx, early 1960s,
rare (fig. 7-50) 150-300

Fig. 7-50: Flintstones Hunting Party playset

Fig. 7-51: Flintstones playset

Fig. 7-52: Record, "Songs of the Flintstones"

Playset, Flintstones, small Marx playset
#2670 . . . . $150-300
Playset, Flintstones, 50 pieces, Marx
playset #4672, 1961 (fig. 7-51) 150-300
Pull toy, Fred plays xylophone,
Fisher-Price, 1962 85-150
Puzzle, Pebbles frame tray puzzle,
Whitman, 1962 10-18
Puzzle set, box of four Children's Puzzles,
10 pieces each, Warren, 1976 10-18
Record 45, picture sleeve, "Goldi-Rocks and
the 3 Bearasauruses," 1961 8-15
Record, 78 RPM, "Songs of the Flintstones,"
picture sleeve, Little Golden Record, 1961
(fig. 7-52) 18-25
Record LP, *Songs of the Flintstones*, 1961 . . 8-15
Record LP, *Flintstones: Original Soundtrack*,
1961 8-15
Slide puzzle, shows Fred, Barney, Wilma,
and Betty, 3" x 3" on 5" x 8" card,
Roalex, 1962 30-50
TV Guide, Fred carves cover logo, June 13,
1964 12-18
Tin wind-up, Fred rides Dino, tin litho,
8.5" long, Marx, 1962 175-250
Tin wind-up, Barney, hops when wound,
tin litho, 3.5", Marx, early 1960s . . . 100-180
Tin wind-up, Dino, hops when wound,
tin litho, 3.5", Marx, early 1960s . . . 100-180
Tin wind-up, Fred, hops when wound,
tin litho, 3.5", Marx, early 1960s . . . 100-180

Trading Cards, Flintstones, Cardz, 1993

Set of 110 cards $14-18
Tekchrome card (one made) 10-12
Hologram card (three different), each 4-6
Unopened box 25-30
Card album $12-15

Trading Cards, Flintstones Movie Cards,
Topps, 1994

Set of 88 cards, 11 stickers $10-15
Flint-Foil card (four different), each 5-7
Unopened box 20-25

Trading Cards, Flintstones: The Movie, Tabb/Edwards,
1994

Set of six promo cards $4-6

Trading Cards, Flintstones NFL
Trading Cards, Cardz, 1993

Set of 110 cards $10-15
Tekchrome card (one made) 8-10
Hologram card (three different), each 4-6
Unopened box 18-22
Four-card promo sheet from Super Bowl . . 8-10
Card album 12-15

Trading Cards, Return of the Flintstones,
Cardz, 1994

Set of 90 cards $9-12
Tekchrome card (three different), each 6-8
Unopened box 20-25
Card album 12-15

Vending Machine, Flintstones Lucky Eggs,
Dino Lays an Egg, 1970s (fig. 7-53) . $250-450

IT'S ABOUT TIME (1966-1967)

Two astronauts break through a time barrier in this
one, and land in a prehistoric village. They make
friends with some of cave people, namely Shad
(Imogene Coca) and her mate Gronk (Joe E. Ross),
and in mid-season, they transport the pair and their
kids back to modern times.

Game, It's About Time, object is to capture
monsters, board game, Ideal, 1967 . $100-150
Lunchbox, steel, dome top, Aladdin,
1967 150-250
Lunch kit thermos, Aladdin, 1967 35-60

Fig. 7-53: Dino Vending Machine

Fig. 7-54: Korg lunchbox with 6" Marx caveman figure

Fig. 7-55: Scarface   **Fig. 7-56:** Stink and Tasha

Fig. 7-57: Pterri

Trading Cards, **It's About Time**, *Topps, 1967*

Note: Test market set, very low distribution
Individual card $20-30
Set (exact number of cards not known)
    rare . . . . no known sales
Wrapper 150-250
Empty box 500-600

KORG: 70,000 B.C. (1974-1975)

This live-action Saturday morning show was produced by Hanna-Barbera and lasted about one year. The show, narrated by Burgess Meredith, focused on the adventures of a struggling Neanderthal family. Jim Malinda starred as Korg.

Game, Korg: 70,000 B.C., board game,
    Milton Bradley, 1974 . . . . $10-18
Lunchbox with thermos, King Seely Thermos
    (shown with Marx figure), 1975
    (fig. 7-54) 35-45

LAND OF THE LOST (1974 -1994)

This Sid and Marty Krofft series originally aired in 1974, and became a recurring Saturday morning staple throughout the 1970s, 1980s, and 1990s, eventually airing on NBC, CBS, and ABC. It tells the story of a forest ranger and his two kids who accidentally travel through time and wind up in prehistory, surrounded by dangerous dinosaurs, a race of ape-like people known as the Pakunis, and an evil race of reptilian people known as the Sleestacks. The 1990s version of the show features a family of three (again a dad and his son and daughter) in the same basic scenario. This time, though, they meet Stink, a primitive monkey creature and Tasha, their new pet reptile.

Action figures and accessories, Tiger Toys, 1992

Annie Porter, 5" $4-8
Boulder Bomber 5-10
Christa, 5" 3-7
Kevin Porter, 5" 3-7
Land Master 8-15
Nim, 5" 2-5
Porter's Treehouse 15-25
Pterodactyl Glider 12-20
S.S. Frisco 8-15
Scarface, electronic T-Rex, boxed
    (fig. 7-55) 12-20
Shung, 5" 2-5
Stink, 5" 2-5
Talking Annie 12-20
Talking Christa 12-20
Talking Kevin 10-15
Talking Shung 20-30
Talking Stink 12-20
Tasha, 5" 4-8
Tom Porter 2-5

Bendee, Stink, carded, JusToys, 1990s
    (fig. 7-56) $3-5
Bendee, Tasha, carded, JusToys, 1990s
    (fig. 7-56) 3-5

PEE WEE'S PLAYHOUSE - PTERRI (1986-1991)

Pee Wee's Pterodactyl friend, Pterri, although somewhat insecure, was one of coolest things on this show—and, this was a really cool show.

Pterri, large plush talking figure,
    Matchbox, 1988 (fig. 7-57) $35-50
Pterri, wind-up figure, Matchbox, 1988 . . . 5-10

Fig. 8-1: T-Rex cookie jar

DINOSAURS
AT HOME

Fig. 8-2: Ceramic cup from Wall Drug

Bank, T-Rex figural, vinyl, Bullyland $10-15

Cookie jar, T-Rex, 10" tall, bought off TV
shopping network, made in China
(fig. 8-1) 35-50

Cup, ceramic, figural Stegosaurus, green and
tan, 6" across 8-12

Cup, ceramic, Wall Drug, South Dakota
promotion, green Brontosaurus figural
(fig. 8-2) 10-15

Juice glass, Brontosaurus, with white
background, 1950s (fig. 8-3) 10-15

Juice glass, New York World's Fair promotion
with Dinoland type and graphics, 1964 . 12-20

Juice glass, Brontosaurus, 4", Welch's
(fig. 8-4) 1-3

Juice glass, Pteranodon, 4", Welch's 1-3

Juice glass, Stegosaurus, 4", Welch's 1-3

Juice glass, Tyrannosaurus, 4", Welch's
(fig. 8-5) 1-3

Memo clip set, soft vinyl, set of 6, Oriental
Trading, 1998, complete set
(figs. 8-6 and 8-7) 4-8

Refrigerator magnet set, 6 different dinosaur
heads, Oriental Trading, 1998, set of 6
(fig. 8-8) 6-10

Salt and pepper shakers, sauropods with
entwining necks, ceramic, year and maker
unknown (fig. 8-9) 20-30

Salt and pepper shakers, Styracosaurus
and Stegosaurus, ceramic, Abbeon,
1960s $45-65

Shampoo bottle, figural Brontosaurus, Avon
(fig. 8-10) 12-20

Shampoo bottle, figural Triceratops, Avon . 12-20

Shampoo bottle, figural T-Rex, Avon 12-20

Fig. 8-3:
Brontosaurus
juice glass

Soft-sculpture Dinosaur pillow kit,
    Dimetrodon, 9" long, by Dinosaur,
    Wheaton, MD, 1975 (fig. 8-11) $15-30
Soft-sculpture Dinosaur pillow kit, Eryops, 5"
    long, by Dinosaur, Wheaton, MD, 1975 . .15-30
Soft-sculpture Dinosaur pillow kit,
    Stegosaurus, 24" long, by Dinosaur,
    Wheaton, MD, 1975 15-30
Soft-sculpture Dinosaur pillow kit, Triceratops,
    6.5" long, by Dinosaur, Wheaton, MD,
    1975 (fig. 8-12) 15-30
Trash Can, black, with colorful dinosaur graphics,
    Chien, 1986 8-12

Fig. 8-4: Brontosaurus juice glass

Fig. 8-5: Tyrannosaurus juice glass

Figs. 8-6 and 8-7: Set of 6 memo clips, from Oriental Trading

Fig. 8-8: Set of 6 refrigerator magnets, from Oriental Trading

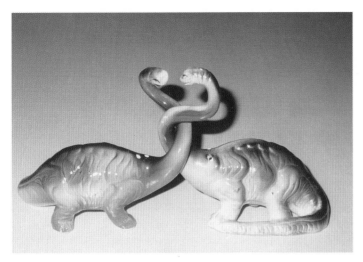

Fig. 8-9: Salt and pepper shakers, unknown manufacturer

Fig. 8-10: Avon shampoo bottle

Fig. 8-11: Dimetrodon pillow kit, by Dinosaur

Fig. 8-12: Triceratops pillow kit, by Dinosaur

SINCLAIR
DINOSAUR COLLECTIBLES

Fig. S-1: Nickel-plated ashtray

Harry F. Sinclair founded what would become the Sinclair Oil Corporation in 1916. Sinclair Oil has long been associated with their Brontosaur mascot. While the dinosaur was initially chosen as their trademark to signify the age of the company's lubricants, it came to mean much more to young and old, becoming an American icon in the 1960s.

Sinclair tried to create a new image for the company in 1959 when they adopted the green "Dino" logo. Prior to that time, the Brontosaurus had been used exclusively to advertise Sinclair lubricants, not the stations. "Dino" was initially used only on store signs, but by the early 1960s, it could be seen on all Sinclair's products and promotions throughout the company's territory. The illuminated, plastic Sinclair sign sporting "Dino" now shone across America, projecting the image of a well-lit, safe, and clean gas station, thus fulfilling Sinclair's advertising goal.

The Sinclair Oil Corporation's association with dinosaurs started in earnest with their elaborate display at the Century of Progress Exhibition (Chicago World's Fair) in 1933 and 1934. Fairgoers could enjoy six mechanical dinosaurs outside Sinclair's pavilion, where smaller dinosaur exhibits were housed. Of course, Dino the Brontosaurus was at the center of the attraction. Sinclair claimed that the oldest crude oil made the finest lubricants and had long used the dinosaur image "to impress upon the minds of motorists the great age of crudes from which Sinclair Motor Oils are refined." The Sinclair Dinosaur Exhibit was designed to further impress this.

Some thirty years later, Sinclair again had a dinosaur exhibit produced for the 1964-1965 New York World's Fair. Sinclair commissioned Paul Jonas, who based his dinosaur sculptures upon the art of Charles R. Knight and used technical advisors Dr. Barnum Brown and Dr. John Ostrom for scientific accuracy.

The Jonas Studio produced nine fiberglass dinosaurs for Sinclair's Dinoland Exhibit. Eight traveled down the Hudson River on a barge while the

Triceratops arrived hanging from a helicopter. The dinosaurs included an enormous Brontosaurus, Struthiomimus, Corythosaurus, Trachodon, Ankylosaurus, Stegosaurus, Triceratops, Ornitholestes, and Tyrannosaurus with motorized lower jaw. Dinoland was the highlight of the fair for the many who have not forgotten it to this day.

Probably one of the most popular dinosaur collectibles associated with Sinclair Oil is the hollow "blow-molded" dinosaurs. For a quarter, machines at the World's Fair would mold a colorful dinosaur figure in a matter of seconds while the customer waited. Though fragile, many of these figures have survived. Other dinosaur collectibles were free giveaways or "premiums," usually for children when their parents came into the station and filled up.

Another popular Sinclair collectible is the company's dinosaur stamps. In 1935, Sinclair gas stations provided their customers with free dinosaur stamp albums. Each week, the Sinclair dealer would offer a different set of dinosaur stamps to go into the album. On the album it read, "The Sinclair dealer will give them out, as long as his supply lasts, to any boy or girl who asks for them, provided he or she is accompanied by an adult."

The 1935 series was issued as a set of twenty-four stamps (eight different blocks of three) plus album. Demand was high and a second print run was necessary. In 1938, Sinclair ran the promotion

again but with completely different stamps and album. The art for the stamps was created by James E. Allen under the supervision of paleontologist Barnum Brown.

The marketing strategy was not resumed again until 1959. Twelve stamps were issued with an album this time. The stamps were in full color with the animal's name on each. Every two weeks for a period of six weeks, Sinclair dealers gave away the stamps needed to fill the album.

Bags of toy dinosaur figures were another Sinclair promotion in the 1960s. Three different size dinosaur toys were given away. One was a small bag of four; the second was a larger bag with two or three times that amount of larger dinosaurs. Both size figures were made by Timmee Toys and were also sold in stores under that name. A third bagged set of dinosaurs by an unknown manufacturer included a full-color brochure on the 1964-1965 World's Fair. The solid, soft plastic dinosaur figures are much in demand by collectors today.

Other dinosaur collectibles from Sinclair include promotionals and any item with the Sinclair "Dino" logo on it: coloring books, signs, oil cans, matchbooks, maps, toy trucks, cups, etc. The following is a list of items most popular with dinosaur figure collectors.

—**Mike Fredericks**

SINCLAIR DINOSAUR COLLECTIBLES VALUE GUIDE

Ashtray, nickel-plated with Dino in center,
    "Go Dino," 7" (fig. S-1) $100-150
Ashtray, plaster with Dino figure,
    "Sinclair," painted 100-150
Ash tray, Dinoland Exhibit with graphics in
    gold paint, square-shaped glass, 1964 . 60-80
Bank, green plastic brontosaurus,
    unmarked, 9" long (fig. S-2) 22-28
Bank, metal figural brontosaurus, "Sinclair"
    on base, 1950s-1960s (fig. S-3) 100-150
Book, The Sinclair Dinosaur Book, 12 pg.
    soft cover book, full color, 1934 20-28
Booklet, "The Exciting World of Dinosaurs,"
    World's Fair version, 1964 (fig. S-4) . . . 20-25

Fig. S-2: Green plastic bank

Fig. S-3: Metal bank

Fig. S-4: World's Fair Booklet

Fig. S-5: Timmee's plastic dinosaur figures

Fig. S-6: Poster depicting SDC's dinosaur figures

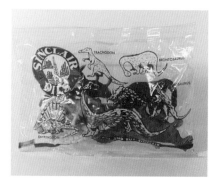

Fig. S-7: SDC's Brontosaurus

Fig. S-8: SDC's carded set with Tyrannosaurus Rex

Fig. S-9: SDC's carded set with Brontosaurus

Booklet, "The Exciting World of Dinosaurs,"
 1967 version,
 (doesn't mention World's Fair) $8-12
Cigarette lighters, metal with gold
 brontosaurus on side, several
 promotional styles, each 25-50
Figure, metal brontosaurus looks backward,
 "Sinclair," wood or marble base,
 1950s-1960s 100-150
Figure, "Dino" as gas station attendant,
 hollow blow-molded plastic, 5" tall,
 originally bagged with header card,
 J.H. Miller Co., extremely rare 250-300
Figures, four dinosaurs/cavemen, 1", bagged,
 "Compliments of your Sinclair Dealer,"
 Timmee Toys, (recent warehouse
 find of these), 1960s 12-18
Figures, plastic dinosaurs, 2", in
 "Sinclair Oils" cellophane header bag,
 Timmee, 1960s (fig. S-5) 35-45

Figures, SDC, carded, 1989-1990s

These dinosaur figures were produced from MPC molds by the Spaulding Dinosaur Company, Kansas, and sold at selected Sinclair gas stations (fig. S-6).
Allosaurus .50¢-1.00
Ankylosaurus . . . . .50¢-1.00
Brontosaurus (fig. S-7) . . . . .50¢-1.00
Cynognathus (sprawled lizard) . . . . . .50¢-1.00
Diatryma .50¢-1.00
Dimetrodon . . . . .50¢-1.00
Macraeuchenia (with hanging nose) . . .50¢-1.00
Megatherium . . . . .50¢-1.00
Parasaurolophus . . . . .50¢-1.00
Smilodon (Saber-Toothed Tiger) . . . . . .50¢-1.00
Stegosaurus . . . . .50¢-1.00
Trachodon . . . . .50¢-1.00
Triceratops . . . . .50¢-1.00
Tyrannosaurus . . . . .50¢-1.00
Woolly Mammoth . . . . .50¢-1.00
Carded set, 4 green plastic animals on blue,
 white, and yellow card, Dino logo, 1990s
 (figs. S-8, S-9) 2-5
Carded set, 4 pastel plastic animals on full-color
 card, Dino logo, 1990s
 (figs. S-10 to S-13) 2-5

*Figures, Sinclair Dinoland World's Fair
promotion, solid color plastic dinosaurs,
3-7", 1964-1965*

Ankylosaurus $4-6
Brontosaurus (fig. S-14) 4-6

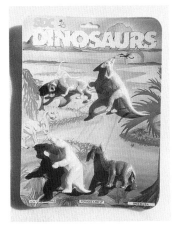

Figs. S-10 to S-13: Various SDC pastel plastic sets

Fig. S-14: Brontosaurus, solid plastic

Fig. S-15: Trachodon, solid plastic

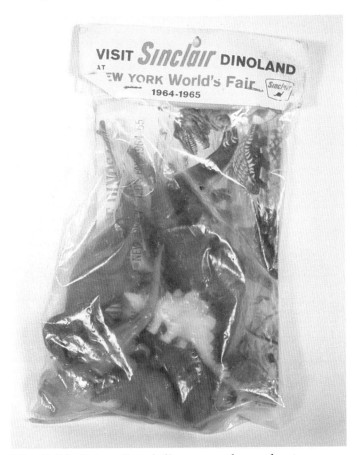

Fig. S-16: Promotional dinosaurs, bagged set

Fig. S-17: Ankylosaurus, hollow plastic

Fig. S-18: Brontosaurus, hollow plastic

Stegosaurus $4-6
Trachodon (fig. S-15) 4-6
Triceratops 4-6
Tyrannosaurus 4-6
Full set, bagged, "Visit Sinclair Dinoland New
  York World's Fair 1964-65," with booklet
  (fig. S-16) .100-150

*Figures, Sinclair Dinoland, hollow, blow-molded waxy
plastic, about 7" long, 1964-1965*

*Note: Some read "Sinclair Dinoland" on base or
"World's Fair 1964-65," with dinosaur's name on
opposite side.*
Ankylosaurus (fig. S-17) $15-25
Brontosaurus, facing forward (fig. S-18) . . 15-25

Fig. S-19: Brontosaurus, facing backward, hollow plastic

Fig. S-20: Corythosaurus, hollow plastic

Fig. S-21: Stegosaurus, hollow plastic

Fig. S-22: Trachodon, hollow plastic

Fig. S-23: Triceratops, hollow plastic

Brontosaurus, facing backward
  (fig. S-19) $15-25
Corythosaurus (fig. S-20) 15-25
Stegosaurus, large 15-25
Stegosaurus, small (fig. S-21) 15-25
Trachodon (fig. S-22) 15-25
Triceratops (fig. S-23) 15-25
Tyrannosaurus Rex (fig. S-24) 15-25

Flags, small, two-color dinosaur flag
on wooden base, calling cards for
Sinclair Service reps, 1950s

Brontosaurus $40-60
Corythosaurus 40-60
Palaeoscincus 40-60
Protoceratops 40-60
Stegosaurus 40-60
Styracosaurus 40-60
Triceratops 40-60
Tyrannosaurus 40-60

Fig. S-24: Tyrannosaurus Rex, hollow plastic

Inflatable dinosaurs, 1960s

Dino, various poses, with or without hat
   (fig. S-25) $12-20
Stegosaurus 10-15
T-Rex 10-15

Juice glass, New York World's Fair promotion
   with Dinoland type and graphics, 1964 . 12-20
Newspapers, Chicago World's Fair free
   newspapers, "Big News" and "Picture News,"
   showing pictures of Sinclair's dinosaur
   exhibit, 1933-1934, each 25-40
Paperweight, figural Dino in gold-colored
   metal, 6" long 100-150
Pin-back button, "Be Prepared," with full
   color Brontosaurus 5-10
Pin-back button, "See the Dinosaurs,"
   with brontosaurus logo 5-10
Pin-back button, "Try Dino," with
   brontosaurus logo 5-10
Sign, round metal Sinclair Dino sign,
   reproduction (fig. S-26) 15-25
Soap, Dino Soap, boxed green "Dino,"
   1960s (fig. S-27) 12-20

Stamp Blocks, 1935

Week 1: Tyrannosaurus, Ornitholestes,
   Parasaurolophus $8-12
Week 2: Mosasaurus, Archaeopteryx,
   Icthyosaurus 8-12
Week 3: Brontosaurus, Monoclonius,
   Stegosaurus (fig. S-28) 8-12
Week 4: Ceratosaurus, Protoceratops,
   Trachodon 8-12
Week 5: Allosaurus, Corythosaurus,
   Camptosaurus 8-12
Week 6: Plesiosaurus, Hesperornis,
   Struthiomimus 8-12
Week 7: Diplodocus, Ankylosaurus,
   Styracosaurus 8-12
Week 8: Palaeoscincus, Pteranodon,
   Triceratops (fig. S-28) 8-12
Album for stamps (fig. S-28) 12-16

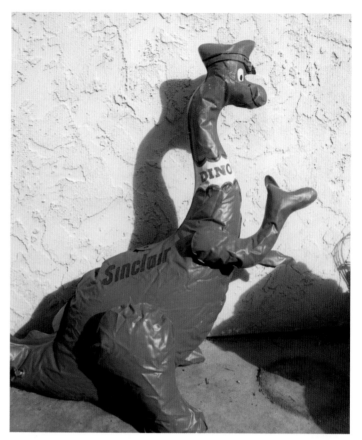

Fig. S-25: Dino

Fig. S-26: Dino sign

Fig. S-27: Dino Soap

Fig. S-28: Stamp album with stamp blocks

Fig. S-29: Stamp strip, week 5 set, 1938

Fig. S-30: Stamp strip, week 6 set, 1938

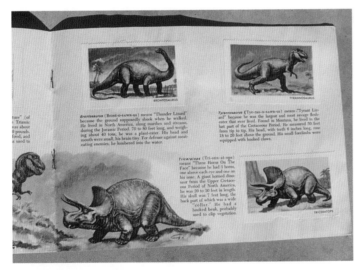

Fig. S-31: Individual stamps, 1959 set

Fig. S-32: Stamp Album, 1959

Fig. 9-1: *Building and Painting Model Dinosaurs*

Fig. 9-7: *Dinosaurs,* Little Golden Book #355

Fig. 9-4: *The Dinosaur Scrapbook*

PAPER
DINOSAURS

BOOKS

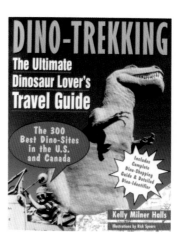

Fig. 9-2: *Dino-Trekking*

Fig. 9-3: *Dinosaur Data Book*

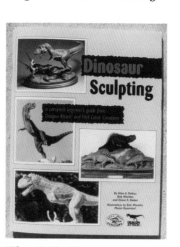

Fig. 9-5: *Dinosaur Sculpting*

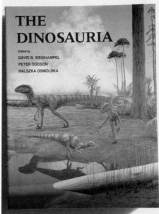

Fig. 9-6: *The Dinosauria*

Fig. 9-8: *Dinosaurs*

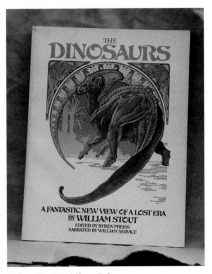

Fig. 9-9: *The Dinosaurs*

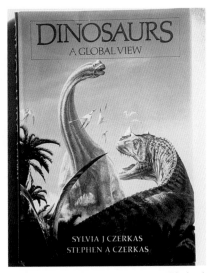

Fig. 9-10: *Dinosaurs: A Global View*

Fig. 9-11: *Dinosaurs and other Prehistoric Beasts*

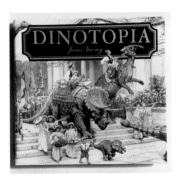

Fig. 9-12: *Dinotopia*

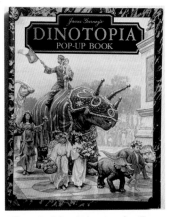

Fig. 9-13: *Dinotopia Pop-Up Book*

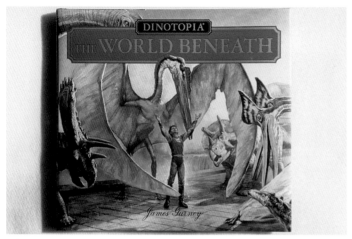

Fig. 9-14: *Dinotopia: The World Beneath*

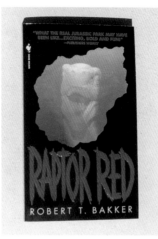

Fig. 9-18: *Raptor Red*

Fig. 9-19: *Tyrannosaurus Rex: The Tyrant King*

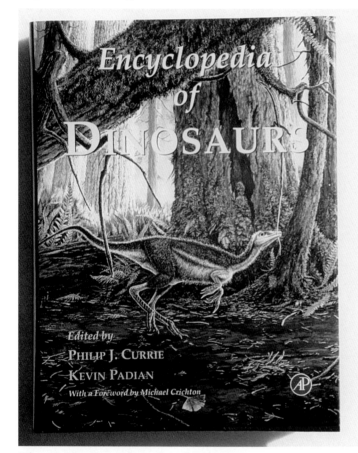

Fig. 9-15: *Encyclopedia of Dinosaurs*

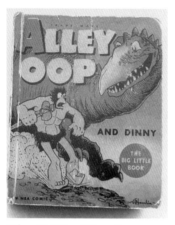

Fig. 9-20: *Alley Oop and Dinny*

Fig. 9-21: *Age of Reptiles,* issue #4

COMICS AND COMIC STRIP CHARACTERS

Alley Oop

Book, *Alley Oop and Dinny,* by V.T. Hamlin,
Big Little Book #763, 1935 (fig. 9-20) . $30-45
Dinosaur hunting license, Alley Oop 25-45
Figure, cloth and fur, 4.5", made for
Newspaper Association members only,
Christy, 1960 60-90

Comic Books, *Age of Reptiles,*
five-comic mini-series, Dark Horse Comics,
each (fig. 9-21) $2-4

Fig. 9-16: *Our Continent*

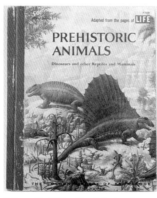

Fig. 9-17: *Prehistoric Animals*

Fig. 9-22: *Fate* magazine

Fig. 9-23: *Fortean Times* magazine

Fig. 9-24: *Prehistoric Times,* issue #14

Fig. 9-25: *Prehistoric Times,* issue #16

MAGAZINES

Dinosaur, photo cover, one issue only, Starlog Communications, 1993 . . . . . . $5-8

Dinosaur, same as above with 3-D cover, Starlog Communications, 1993 6-12

Dinosaur Delirium, one issue only, Starline Publications, 1993 6-9

Fate, cover story, "Did Man Tame the Dinosaur?" Feb./Mar. 1952 (fig. 9-22) . . .8-12

Fortean Times, #83, cover story, "Dinosaurs Alive!" May 1996 (fig. 9-23) . . .4-6

Life, "The World We Live In," Zallinger dinosaur cover and mural, Sept. 7, 1953 .8-12

Life, "The World We Live In," Zallinger prehistoric mammal cover and mural, Oct. 19, 1953 7-10

Life, Zallinger cover, prehistoric South America, Jan. 26, 1959 7-10

Prehistoric Times, *magazine for dinosaur collectors and enthusiasts, edited by Mike Fredericks*

#1, sold out $15-25
#2, sold out 15-20
#3, sold out 12-18
#4, sold out 12-18
#5, sold out 12-18
#6, sold out 12-18
#7, sold out 12-18
#8, sold out 12-18
#9, sold out 12-18
#10, sold out 12-18
#11, sold out 12-18
#12, sold out 12-18
#13, sold out $12-18

Fig. 9-26: *Prehistoric Times,* issue #22

#14 (fig. 9-24) 10-15
#15 10-15
#16 (fig. 9-25) 10-15
#17 10-15
#18 10-15
#19 10-15
#20 10-15
#21 10-15
#22 (fig. 9-26) 10-15
#23 (fig. 9-27) 6-9
#24 (fig. 9-28) $6-9

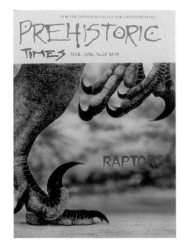

Fig. 9-27: *Prehistoric Times*, issue #23

Fig. 9-28: *Prehistoric Times*, issue #24

Fig. 9-29: *Prehistoric Times*, issue #25

Fig. 9-30: *Prehistoric Times*, issue #25

Fig. 9-32: *Prehistoric Times*, issue #32

Fig. 9-33: *Prehistoric Times*, issue #33

Fig. 9-31: *Prehistoric Times*, issue #26

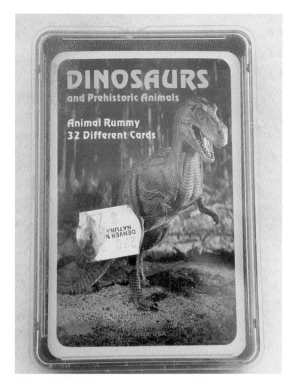

Fig. 9-34: Dinosaur Animal Rummy

Fig. 9-35: Cigarette cards

Fig. 9-36: Edu-Cards' flash cards

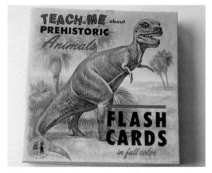

Fig. 9-37: McGraw Hill's flash cards

Fig. 9-38: Allosaurus scene postcard, front

Fig. 9-39: Allosaurus scene postcard, back

Fig. 9-40: Brontosaurus scene postcard

TRADING CARDS, STICKERS, PLAYING CARDS, POST CARDS, & FLASH CARDS

Card game, Dinosaur Animal Rummy,
Safari Ltd. (fig. 9-34) $4-8
Cigarette cards, European, 1950s or 1960s,
each (fig. 9-35) 2-5
Flash cards, Dinosaurs and Prehistoric
Animals, Edu-Cards, 1975 (fig. 9-36) . . . 8-12
Flash cards, Teach Me About Prehistoric
Animals, McGraw Hill, 1960 (fig. 9-37) . 12-20

Postcards, Giant Postcards from painting at American Museum of Natural History, Dexter Press

Allosaurus scene (figs. 9-38 and 9-39) $3-6
Brontosaurus scene (fig. 9-40) 3-6
Postcards, pretty pastel dinosaur scenes,
perforated edges, year & maker unknown,
each (figs. 9-41 to 9-46) 2-4
Sticker, Dinosaur National Monument souvenir,
1950s (fig. 9-47) 4-8
Stickers, Dinosaurs Album Stickers, set of
150 stickers and album, Diamond,
1992 12-16
Stickers, Wacko-Saurs, set of 48 stickers,
Diamond, 1987 10-12

*Trading Cards, Deanosaurs Collector Cards,
by Dean Walker, 1996-present*

*These great cards picture items from the collection of
Dean Walker, fully describing each item.*

Series A, 18 cards $6-10
Series B, 18 cards 6-10
Series C, 18 cards 6-10
Series D, 18 cards, picturing only dinosaur
    species his wife, Janice, could name 6-10
Series E, 18 cards, picturing only dinosaurs
    his wife could never in a billion years
    name 6-10
Series F, 18 cards, focusing on figures
    produced in England, Germany, and
    Austria (fig. 9-48) 6-10
Series G, 18 cards, picturing his kids' favorite
    pieces from the collection 6-10
Series H, 18 cards, all prehistoric elephant
    figures 6-10
Series I, 18 cards, all resin dinosaur
    model kits 6-10

Figs. 9-41 to 9-46: Assorted pastel postcards

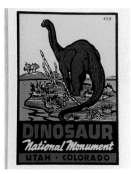

Fig. 9-47: Souvenir
sticker

Fig. 9-48: Deanosaurus
Collector Cards, Series F

Fig. 9-49: Dinosaur hatchling trading card, Dino Cards

Fig. 9-50: Tyrannosaurus trading card, Dino Cards

Fig. 9-51: Rhamphorhynchus trading card, Dino Cards

Fig. 9-52: Pachycephalosaurus trading card, Dino Cards

Fig. 9-53: Triceratops trading card, Dino Cards

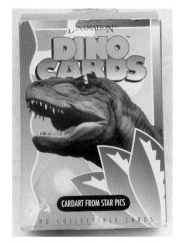

Fig. 9-54: Dino Cards' 80-card set

Trading Cards, Dino Cards/Dinamation, Star Pics, 1992

Set of 80 cards (figs. 9-49 to 9-54) $10-14

Trading Cards, Dino Cardz, 1992

Set of 50 regular cards (figs. 9-55 to 9-57) . $4-8
Set of 80 UV-coated cards 6-10
Unopened box 15-30

Trading Cards, Dino Cardz Head Set, 1992

Full set (figs. 9-58 to 9-60) $6-12

Trading Cards, Dinosaur Nation, Kitchen Sink, 1993

Boxed set of 36 cards $10-12

Trading Cards, Dinosaurs, Illuminations, 1987

Series 1-12 (5 cards per series, each packaged
separately), each $3-5

Trading Cards, Dinosaurs, First Glance Productions, 1993

Set of 24 cards $7-10
Hologram mail order card 12-15
Unopened box 22-26

Fig. 9-56: Kronosaurus trading card, Dino Cardz

Fig. 9-57: Protoceratops trading card, Dino Cardz

Fig. 9-55: Coelophysis trading card, Dino Cardz

Fig. 9-61: Assortment of Nu-Cards Sales' trading cards

Fig. 9-58: Corythosaurus trading card, Dino Cardz

Fig. 9-62: Nu-Cards' trading card pack

Fig. 9-59: Dilophosaurus trading card, Dino Cardz

Fig. 9-60: Plateosaurus trading card, Dino Cardz

Fig. 9-63: Topps' trading card set

Fig. 9-65: Dinotopia trading card

Fig. 9-66: Dinotopia trading card

Fig. 9-64: Topps' trading cards

Fig. 9-67: Albertosaurus trading card, Mesozoic Set

Fig. 9-68: Dilophosaurus trading card, Mesozoic Set

Fig. 9-69: Rhabdodon trading card, Mesozoic Set

Trading Cards, Golden Press, perforated edges, year unknown

Individual card $1-2
Full set 30-50

Trading Cards, Dinosaurs, Nu-Cards Sales, 1961

Individual cards (fig. 9-61) each $3-5
Set of 80 cards 350-400
Unopened pack (fig. 9-62) 25-30
Unopened box 600-650

Trading Cards, Dinosaurs, Milwaukee Museum, 1983-1989

Sets released yearly 1983-1989, each
    containing 4 to 8 cards, each set $2-3

Trading Cards, Dinosaurs Attack, Topps, 1998 (take-off of Mars Attacks set)

Set of 55 cards, 11 stickers (figs. 9-63
    and 9-64) $12-15

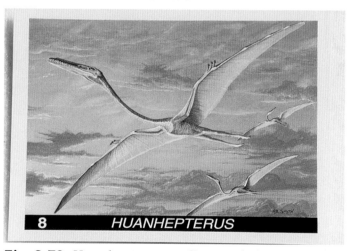

Fig. 9-70: Huanhepterus trading card, Cottage Cards

Fig. 9-71: Pterodaustro trading card, Cottage Cards

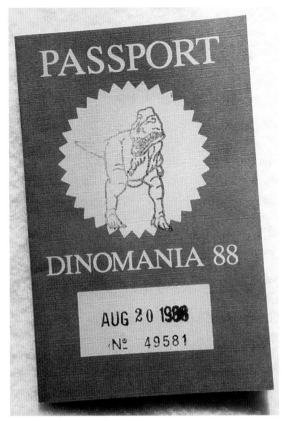

Fig. 9-72: Dinomania '88 Passport

Fig. 9-75: Zallinger Mural Poster, first piece

Fig. 9-76: Zallinger Mural Poster, second piece

Fig. 9-73: Dinosaur Discovery Learning Kit

Fig. 9-74: Dinosaur Mad Libs

Trading Cards, Pterosaurs, series of prehistoric flying reptile cards, Cottage Cards, 1994
(figs. 9-70 and 9-71)

Full set $8-12

Miscellaneous Paper Dinosaur Collectibles

Dinomania '88 Passport, from Idaho Museum
of Natural History, 1988 (fig. 9-72) $2-5
Dinosaur Discovery Learning Kit, with rubber
stamps, fact book, etc., Cobblehill Books,
1990s (fig. 9-73) 8-15
Dinosaur Mad Libs, book of word games,
Price Stern Sloan, 1993 (fig. 9-74) 2-4
Iron-on Transfers, "Dig a Dinosaur," Celia
Totus Enterprises, ... 2-5
Zallinger Mural Poster, from *Life* magazine,
in two pieces, My Weekly Reader, 1968
(figs. 9-75 and 9-76) 30-50

Trading Cards, Dinotopia, Collect-A-Card, 1995
(figs. 9-65 and 9-66)

Set of 72 cards (figs. 9-65 and 9-66) $8-12
Dinofold card (6 different), each 5-7
Dinovision card (8 different), each 7-9
Dinovision large print 28-32
Unopened box 28-32

*Trading Cards, Mesozoic Dinosaur Card Set,
Redstone Marketing Inc.*

Set of 46 cards (figs. 9-67 to 9-69) $5-10

DINOSAUR DIRECTORY
AN A-TO-Z OF PREHISTORIC CREATURES

Allosaurus (al'ə sôr'əs)
Allosaurus was a large carnivorous dinosaur, very common in the late Jurassic period. Its fossils have been found in North America, Africa, and Australia. Technically translated to mean "Different Lizard," Allosaurus was about thirty-five to forty feet long and weighed one and a half tons. Gwangi, in The Valley of Gwangi, was an Allosaurus.

Anatosaurus (ə nat'ə sôr'əs)
Formerly known as "Trachodon," this Cretaceous-era duck-billed dinosaur was the first to be discovered in the United States (near Philadelphia). Measuring about thirty-five to forty feet long, Anatosaurus walked on two legs and had webbed feet. An excellent swimmer, Anatosaurus was also equipped with about 2,000 small teeth, hiding behind his benign-looking ducky bill.

Ankylosaurus (ang'kə lō sôr'əs)
This short-legged, spiky dinosaur has developed a large fan base. Abundant in North America's late Cretaceous period, the Ankylosaurus ("curved lizard") was about thirty-five feet long. Its tail ended in a bony club, and it was perhaps the best-protected dinosaur ever—basically a walking bone- and spike-covered tank. The Japanese movie monster, Angilas, was loosely modeled after the Ankylosaurus.

Apatosaurus (ə pat'ə sôr'əs)
Formerly known as the "Brontosaurus," this dinosaur lived in the west-central United States during the late Jurassic period. Apatosaurus was a vegetarian, weighing in at more than twenty tons, and measuring up to seventy feet long with its enormous tail. It is probably the best known sauropod.

Archaeopteryx (är'kē op'tə riks)
Believed to be the first real bird, this feathered dinosaur's name means "ancient wing." Its remains, from the late Jurassic period, have been found in Bavaria and Germany. Archaeopteryx was about two to three feet long, and it had sharp teeth, and long claws on its wings. It is unique in the dinosaur registry.

Brachiosaurus (brā'kē ə sôr'əs)
Brachiosaurus got around a bit, as his fossils have turned up in locations as far apart as Colorado and Tanzania. This large sauropod is easily identified by its signature head shape, with its nostrils up on top. It is one of the tallest dinosaurs, measuring up to fifty-two feet tall. It has a relatively short tail, and the general appearance of a very steep slope.

Brontosaurus (bron'tə sôr'əs)
See Apatosaurus.

Brontotherium (bron'tə thēr'ē əm)
An ancestor of our own rhinoceros, this animal's name literally means "giant." He was about eight feet tall—all bulk and a very small brain. His most distinguishing feature is the "Y"-shaped horn protruding from the top of his nose. Brontotherium lived in North America and the Balkans.

Camarasaurus (kə mâr'ə sôr'əs)
This stocky sauropod wandered the western United States during the late Jurassic period. Weighing as much as twenty tons and measuring up to sixty feet long, Camarasaurus literally means "chambered lizard."

Cave Bear
Cave Bears were a little bigger than modern brown bears, and lived primarily off plants and fruits. They went into caves to hibernate, give birth, and die. In Europe, Cave Bears became extinct before the end of the Ice Age, probably at least partly because prehistoric people hunted them for food and fur.

Ceratosaurus (ser'ə tə sôr'əs)
The translated name, "horned lizard," refers to this meat-eater's short bony stumps protruding above its eyes and nose. Found in North America and East Africa during the late Jurassic period, Ceratosaurus was nearly eighteen feet long, stood on two legs, and had short bony plates running the length of its back.

Coelodonta (Woolly Rhino) (sē'lə don'tə)
This Ice Age vegetarian was probably hunted to extinction by prehistoric man about 10,000 years ago in Europe and Asia. Measuring about fifteen feet long, the Coelodonta had two horns on its nose and was covered with wool and long bristly hair. Its name means "antique."

Corythosaurus (kō rith'ə sôr'əs)
This Canadian plant-eating dinosaur has a sort of second nose in a rounded crest on top of its head, and a toothless beak. Some believe he was able to hide in deep water and breathe through the top of his head. From the Latin for "helmet lizard," Corythosaurus lived during the late Cretaceous period.

Diatryma (dī'ə trē'mə)
This giant bird stood at more than six feet tall and had a head nearly as big as a horse's head. Its wings were useless, but its powerful beak, fast ground speed, and huge claws enabled it to be a successful predator. Diatryma lived on the plains of North America and Europe during the early Tertiary period. "Diatryma" means "through a hole."

Dilophosaurus (dī lôf'ə sôr'əs)
Fossil discoveries in Arizona have helped identify this two-legged meat eater of the early Jurassic period. Its chief distinguishing feature is a pair of parallel curved ridges extending from its nose to the back of its head. In *Jurassic Park*, Dilophosaurus was outfitted with a lovely, decorative neck frill, and had the ability to spit poison at its enemies.

Dimetrodon (dī me'trə don')
One of the staples of early prehistoric films (because he looks like a lizard with a fin attached to his back), Dimetrodon lived in North America in Permian times. He was about seven to ten feet long, ate meat, and was probably the fastest reptile of his time. He is not technically a dinosaur, but a mammal-like reptile.

Diplodocus (di plod'ə kəs)
More slender and elongated than its close relative, the Apatosaurus, Diplodocus is one of the best-known sauropods. It roamed the Rocky Mountain region during the late Jurassic period, and could reach lengths exceeding eighty feet. Its brain, however, was very small, even by dinosaur standards. "Diplodocus" translates to mean "double beam."

Eryops (ēr'ē ops)
This ten- to twelve-foot amphibian roamed the beaches of the Permian period. A stocky species, Eryops weighed more than two hundred pounds, and ate crab and fish.

Eusthenopteron (yōō'thin op'tə ron)
It looks like a fish, but it was actually a sort of amphibian—the first to be able to live on land for a short period. This creature is the one that started the march of life onto land, way back in the Devonian period. It was about two feet long.

Gorgosaurus (gôr'gə sôr'əs)
The real Gorgosaurus only slightly resembles its cinematic namesake, "Gorgo," lacking the frilled ears and oversized hands. It was, in actuality, a gigantic relative of the Tyrannosaurus, and it lived in Canada during the late Cretaceous period.

Hadrosaurus (had'rə sôr'əs)
This popular duck-billed dinosaur roamed North America during the late Cretaceous period. Its name means "big lizard," and Hadrosaurus probably alternated between walking on two and four feet.

Ichthyosaurus (ik'thē ə sôr'əs)
This prehistoric "fish-lizard" sported fins and a vertical tail. Technically a marine reptile, it existed through most of the Triassic and Cretaceous periods.

Iguanodon (i gwä'nə don')
Fossil remains of Iguanodon have been found in North America, Europe, and Asia. Abundant in the early Cretaceous period, Iguanodon measured up to thirty feet long, and could weigh as much as five tons. It walked on two legs, and its name means "tooth lizard." Iguanodon fossils were first unearthed in Sussex, England, in 1822, when it became the first scientifically named dinosaur.

Irish Elk (Megaloceros) (meg'ə los'ər əs)
Fossilized antlers of this prehistoric deer have measured up to thirteen feet across and weighed more than seventy-five pounds. This beast stood about six or seven feet tall at the shoulder, and no evidence suggests that it was hunted by prehistoric people. Megaloceros lived in Europe and Asia during the Quaternary period, and became extinct just 12,000 years ago.

Lambeosaurus (lam'bē ə sôr'əs)

This duck-billed plant eater is distinguished by its mushroom-shaped head crest. It grew up to fifty feet long, and is known to have roamed western Mexico, California, and Canada.

Megatherium (Giant Ground Sloth)
(meg'ə thēr'ē əm)

Picture an elephant-sized sloth. Standing up to twenty feet tall, this creature has been commemorated in many classic prehistoric toy lines. It lived in North and South America, and is listed among the many Ice Age casualties.

Mosasaurus (mōs'ə sôr'əs)

These eel-like marine reptiles could measure more than thirty feet long, and they swam in the late Cretaceous period.

Nanosaurus (nan'ə sôr'əs)

This "dwarf lizard" sprinted around Colorado and Utah during the late Jurassic period. Measuring only about a yard long, this plant-eater walked on its hind legs.

Pachycephalosaurus (pak'i sef'ə lə sôr'əs)

Distinguished by its large bony domed head and spiky snout, this two-legged plant-eater roamed Canada and the northern United States during the late Cretaceous period. Its name means, literally, "thick-nosed lizard."

Parasaurolophus (par'ə sôr'ə lof'əs)

This duck-billed dinosaur is easily recognized by the five-foot-long hollow blunt horn that projected backward off its face. It is sometimes shown with a frill or web connecting the horn to the back of its neck. Remains have been found in Canada, Utah, and New Mexico. Parasaurolophus grew up to thirty-five feet long.

Plateosaurus (plat'e ə sôr'əs)

Looking somewhat like a cross between a sauropod and a theropod, Plateosaurus had a long neck and stood on its hind legs. Measuring from about ten to twenty feet long, it thrived during the Triassic period, eating both meat and plants in the warm, swampy areas of Europe and Asia. Its name means "flat lizard."

Plesiosaurus (plē'sē ə sôr'əs)

These carnivorous marine reptiles thrived in the Mesozoic era. Sporting four strong flippers and long necks, they measured up to forty feet long. By the Jurassic period, Plesiosaurs were found in all of Earth's oceans. Some theorize that the Loch Ness Monster is a surviving Plesiosaurus.

Protoceratops (prot'ə sar'ə tops)

The name means "first horned face," and this late Cretaceous dinosaur was just that, as far as we know. Found in China, Mongolia, and North America, this four-legged vegetarian had a sharp, curved beak and a wide bony neck frill. He measured about six or seven feet long, and frequently topped two hundred pounds.

Pteranodon (tə ran'ə don')

This popular Pterosaur thrived in North America and Europe during the Cretaceous period. With a wingspan that could top twenty-five feet, the Pteranodon had a distinguishing long bony crest on top of its head. Unlike some other flying reptiles, it had no tail. It may have been warm-blooded, and its name means "wing without teeth."

Quetzalcoatlus (ket säl'kō ät'ləs)

Discovered in 1971, Quetzalcoatlus shocked scientists with a wingspan of nearly forty feet. This gigantic predator lived in the southwestern United States during the late Cretaceous period, and was named after a Mexican mythological creature.

Saltopus (sôl'tə pus)

This tiny predator lived in Scotland during the late Triassic period. Possibly the oldest European dinosaur, Saltopus weighed just two pounds, and stood only about two feet tall. Its name means "leaping foot."

Smilodon (Saber-Toothed Tiger) (smī'lə don')

He's not called "Smilodon" because he was happy. The name actually means "carving knife." One of the most beloved of all prehistoric mammals, the saber-toothed tiger prowled North America during the Ice Age (Quaternary period). About the size of a modern-day lion, Smilodon used his enormous fangs to pierce the tough skin of his victims.